D1823177

Web Technologies and APIs
Complete Self-Assessment Guide

The guidance in this Self-Assessment is based on Web Technologies and APIs best practices and standards in business process architecture, design and quality management. The guidance is also based on the professional judgment of the individual collaborators listed in the Acknowledgments.

Copyright © by The Art of Service
http://theartofservice.com
service@theartofservice.com

Table of Contents

About The Art of Service

The Art of Service, Business Process Architects since 2000, is dedicated to helping stakeholders achieve excellence.

Defining, designing, creating, and implementing a process to solve a stakeholders challenge or meet an objective is the most valuable role... In EVERY group, company, organization and department.

Unless you're talking a one-time, single-use project, there should be a process. Whether that process is managed and implemented by humans, AI, or a combination of the two, it needs to be designed by someone with a complex enough perspective to ask the right questions.

Someone capable of asking the right questions and step back and say, 'What are we really trying to accomplish here? And is there a different way to look at it?'

With The Art of Service's Standard Requirements Self-Assessments, we empower people who can do just that — whether their title is marketer, entrepreneur, manager, salesperson, consultant, Business Process Manager, executive assistant, IT Manager, CIO etc... —they are the people who rule the future. They are people who watch the process as it happens, and ask the right questions to make the process work better.

Contact us when you need any support with this Self-Assessment and any help with templates, blue-prints and examples of standard documents you might need:

http://theartofservice.com
service@theartofservice.com

Acknowledgments

This checklist was developed under the auspices of The Art of Service, chaired by Gerardus Blokdyk.

Representatives from several client companies participated in the preparation of this Self-Assessment.

Our deepest gratitude goes out to Matt Champagne, Ph.D. Surveys Expert, for his invaluable help and advise in structuring the Self Assessment.

In addition, we are thankful for the design and printing services provided.

Included Resources - how to access

Included with your purchase of the book is the Web Technologies and APIs Self-Assessment Spreadsheet Dashboard which contains all questions and Self-Assessment areas and auto-generates insights, graphs, and project RACI planning - all with examples to get you started right away.

How? Simply send an email to
access@theartofservice.com
with this books' title in the subject to get the Web Technologies and APIs Self Assessment Tool right away.

You will receive the following contents with New and Updated specific criteria:
- The latest quick edition of the book in PDF
- The latest complete edition of the book in PDF, which criteria correspond to the criteria in...
- The Self-Assessment Excel Dashboard, and...
- Example pre-filled Self-Assessment Excel Dashboard to get familiar with results generation
- ...plus an extra, special, resource that helps you with project managing.

INCLUDES LIFETIME SELF ASSESSMENT UPDATES

Every self assessment comes with Lifetime Updates and Lifetime Free Updated Books. Lifetime Updates is an industry-first feature which allows you to receive verified self assessment updates, ensuring you always have the most accurate information at your fingertips.

Get it now- you will be glad you did - do it now, before you forget.

Send an email to **access@theartofservice.com** with this books' title in the subject to get the Web Technologies and APIs Self Assessment Tool right away.

Your feedback is invaluable to us

If you recently bought this book, we would love to hear from you! You can do this by writing a review on amazon (or the online store where you purchased this book) about your last purchase! As part of our continual service improvement process, we love to hear real client experiences and feedback.

How does it work?
To post a review on Amazon, just log in to your account and click on the Create Your Own Review button (under Customer Reviews) of the relevant product page. You can find examples of product reviews in Amazon. If you purchased from another online store, simply follow their procedures.

What happens when I submit my review?
Once you have submitted your review, send us an email at review@theartofservice.com with the link to your review so we can properly thank you for your feedback.

Purpose of this Self-Assessment

This Self-Assessment has been developed to improve understanding of the requirements and elements of Web Technologies and APIs, based on best practices and standards in business process architecture, design and quality management.

It is designed to allow for a rapid Self-Assessment to determine how closely existing management practices and procedures correspond to the elements of the Self-Assessment.

The criteria of requirements and elements of Web Technologies and APIs have been rephrased in the format of a Self-Assessment questionnaire, with a seven-criterion scoring system, as explained in this document.

In this format, even with limited background knowledge of Web

Technologies and APIs, a manager can quickly review existing operations to determine how they measure up to the standards. This in turn can serve as the starting point of a 'gap analysis' to identify management tools or system elements that might usefully be implemented in the organization to help improve overall performance.

How to use the Self-Assessment

On the following pages are a series of questions to identify to what extent your Web Technologies and APIs initiative is complete in comparison to the requirements set in standards.

To facilitate answering the questions, there is a space in front of each question to enter a score on a scale of '1' to '5'.

1 Strongly Disagree

2 Disagree

3 Neutral

4 Agree

5 Strongly Agree

Read the question and rate it with the following in front of mind:

'In my belief, the answer to this question is clearly defined'.

There are two ways in which you can choose to interpret this statement;
1. how aware are you that the answer to the question is clearly defined
2. for more in-depth analysis you can choose to gather

evidence and confirm the answer to the question. This obviously will take more time, most Self-Assessment users opt for the first way to interpret the question and dig deeper later on based on the outcome of the overall Self-Assessment.

A score of '1' would mean that the answer is not clear at all, where a '5' would mean the answer is crystal clear and defined. Leave emtpy when the question is not applicable or you don't want to answer it, you can skip it without affecting your score. Write your score in the space provided.

After you have responded to all the appropriate statements in each section, compute your average score for that section, using the formula provided, and round to the nearest tenth. Then transfer to the corresponding spoke in the Web Technologies and APIs Scorecard on the second next page of the Self-Assessment.

Your completed Web Technologies and APIs Scorecard will give you a clear presentation of which Web Technologies and APIs areas need attention.

Web Technologies and APIs Scorecard Example

Example of how the finalized Scorecard can look like:

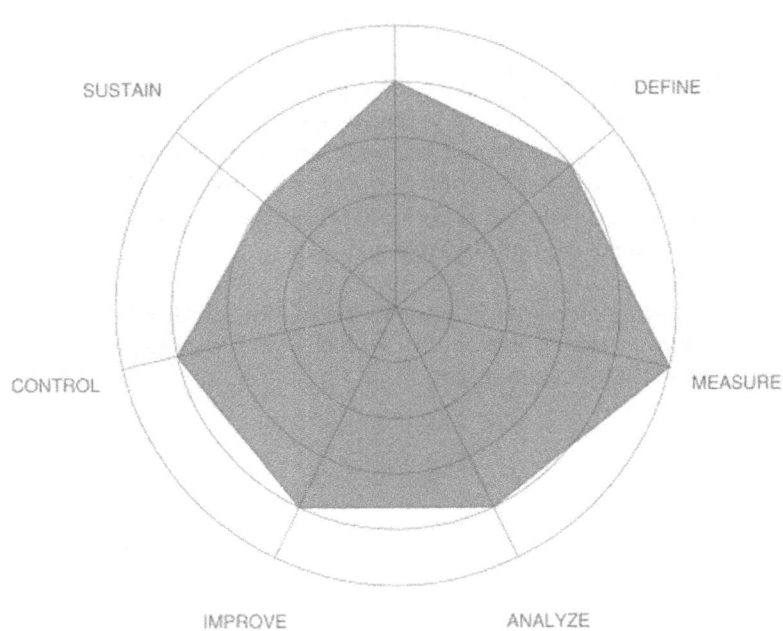

RECOGNIZE

SUSTAIN

DEFINE

CONTROL

MEASURE

IMPROVE

ANALYZE

Web Technologies and APIs Scorecard

Your Scores:

BEGINNING OF THE SELF-ASSESSMENT:

CRITERION #1: RECOGNIZE

INTENT: Be aware of the need for change. Recognize that there is an unfavorable variation, problem or symptom.

In my belief, the answer to this question is clearly defined:

5 Strongly Agree

4 Agree

3 Neutral

2 Disagree

1 Strongly Disagree

1. What tools and technologies are needed for a custom Web Technologies and APIs project?
<--- Score

2. How do you assess your Web Technologies and APIs workforce capability and capacity needs, including skills, competencies, and staffing levels?
<--- Score

3. What are the expected benefits of Web Technologies and APIs to the business?
<--- Score

4. What is the smallest subset of the problem you can usefully solve?
<--- Score

5. Think about the people you identified for your Web Technologies and APIs project and the project responsibilities you would assign to them. what kind of training do you think they would need to perform these responsibilities effectively?
<--- Score

6. What information do users need?
<--- Score

7. Who else hopes to benefit from it?
<--- Score

8. Will Web Technologies and APIs deliverables need to be tested and, if so, by whom?
<--- Score

9. Will it solve real problems?
<--- Score

10. Does Web Technologies and APIs create potential expectations in other areas that need to be recognized and considered?
<--- Score

11. Who defines the rules in relation to any given issue?
<--- Score

12. For your Web Technologies and APIs project, identify and describe the business environment, is there more than one layer to the business environment?
<--- Score

13. What prevents you from making the changes you know will make you a more effective Web Technologies and APIs leader?
<--- Score

14. What would happen if Web Technologies and APIs weren't done?
<--- Score

15. How are the Web Technologies and APIs's objectives aligned to the organization's overall business strategy?
<--- Score

16. What are your needs in relation to Web Technologies and APIs skills, labor, equipment, and markets?
<--- Score

17. What does Web Technologies and APIs success mean to the stakeholders?
<--- Score

18. Are there Web Technologies and APIs problems defined?
<--- Score

19. Who needs to know about Web Technologies and APIs?

<--- Score

20. Will new equipment/products be required to facilitate Web Technologies and APIs delivery, for example is new software needed?
<--- Score

21. How do you take a forward-looking perspective in identifying Web Technologies and APIs research related to market response and models?
<--- Score

22. How much are sponsors, customers, partners, stakeholders involved in Web Technologies and APIs? In other words, what are the risks, if Web Technologies and APIs does not deliver successfully?
<--- Score

23. Do you know what you need to know about Web Technologies and APIs?
<--- Score

24. How can auditing be a preventative security measure?
<--- Score

25. What else needs to be measured?
<--- Score

26. What do you need to start doing?
<--- Score

27. What training and capacity building actions are needed to implement proposed reforms?
<--- Score

28. Does your organization need more Web Technologies and APIs education?
<--- Score

29. Consider your own Web Technologies and APIs project, what types of organizational problems do you think might be causing or affecting your problem, based on the work done so far?
<--- Score

30. As a sponsor, customer or management, how important is it to meet goals, objectives?
<--- Score

31. What are the business objectives to be achieved with Web Technologies and APIs?
<--- Score

32. Can management personnel recognize the monetary benefit of Web Technologies and APIs?
<--- Score

33. Is it clear when you think of the day ahead of you what activities and tasks you need to complete?
<--- Score

34. Are controls defined to recognize and contain problems?
<--- Score

35. How does it fit into your organizational needs and tasks?
<--- Score

36. Will a response program recognize when a crisis occurs and provide some level of response?

<--- Score

37. What situation(s) led to this Web Technologies and APIs Self Assessment?
<--- Score

38. Who had the original idea?
<--- Score

39. What should be considered when identifying available resources, constraints, and deadlines?
<--- Score

40. What vendors make products that address the Web Technologies and APIs needs?
<--- Score

41. Are there any specific expectations or concerns about the Web Technologies and APIs team, Web Technologies and APIs itself?
<--- Score

42. Have you identified your Web Technologies and APIs key performance indicators?
<--- Score

43. Are there recognized Web Technologies and APIs problems?
<--- Score

44. What problems are you facing and how do you consider Web Technologies and APIs will circumvent those obstacles?
<--- Score

45. How are you going to measure success?

<--- Score

46. How do you identify the kinds of information that you will need?
<--- Score

47. When a Web Technologies and APIs manager recognizes a problem, what options are available?
<--- Score

Add up total points for this section:
_ _ _ _ _ = Total points for this section

Divided by: _ _ _ _ _ _ (number of statements answered) = _ _ _ _ _ _ Average score for this section

Transfer your score to the Web Technologies and APIs Index at the beginning of the Self-Assessment.

CRITERION #2: DEFINE:

INTENT: Formulate the business problem. Define the problem, needs and objectives.

In my belief, the answer to this question is clearly defined:

5 Strongly Agree

4 Agree

3 Neutral

2 Disagree

1 Strongly Disagree

1. Are there different segments of customers?
<--- Score

2. Is there a critical path to deliver Web Technologies and APIs results?
<--- Score

3. Is Web Technologies and APIs linked to key business goals and objectives?

<--- Score

4. Have the customer needs been translated into specific, measurable requirements? How?
<--- Score

5. Are approval levels defined for contracts and supplements to contracts?
<--- Score

6. Are customers identified and high impact areas defined?
<--- Score

7. What defines best in class?
<--- Score

8. If substitutes have been appointed, have they been briefed on the Web Technologies and APIs goals and received regular communications as to the progress to date?
<--- Score

9. Do you all define Web Technologies and APIs in the same way?
<--- Score

10. Is the scope of Web Technologies and APIs defined?
<--- Score

11. How will variation in the actual durations of each activity be dealt with to ensure that the expected Web Technologies and APIs results are met?
<--- Score

12. What specifically is the problem? Where does it occur? When does it occur? What is its extent?
<--- Score

13. Is it clearly defined in and to your organization what you do?
<--- Score

14. Has a team charter been developed and communicated?
<--- Score

15. How would you define the culture at your organization, how susceptible is it to Web Technologies and APIs changes?
<--- Score

16. Is Web Technologies and APIs currently on schedule according to the plan?
<--- Score

17. Are task requirements clearly defined?
<--- Score

18. How can the value of Web Technologies and APIs be defined?
<--- Score

19. Has a high-level 'as is' process map been completed, verified and validated?
<--- Score

20. Is the current 'as is' process being followed? If not, what are the discrepancies?
<--- Score

21. Has the improvement team collected the 'voice of the customer' (obtained feedback – qualitative and quantitative)?
<--- Score

22. How do you keep key subject matter experts in the loop?
<--- Score

23. What are the rough order estimates on cost savings/opportunities that Web Technologies and APIs brings?
<--- Score

24. Will team members regularly document their Web Technologies and APIs work?
<--- Score

25. What are the Roles and Responsibilities for each team member and its leadership? Where is this documented?
<--- Score

26. Has a project plan, Gantt chart, or similar been developed/completed?
<--- Score

27. What key business process output measure(s) does Web Technologies and APIs leverage and how?
<--- Score

28. Is there a completed, verified, and validated high-level 'as is' (not 'should be' or 'could be') business process map?
<--- Score

29. Are improvement team members fully trained on Web Technologies and APIs?
<--- Score

30. Are audit criteria, scope, frequency and methods defined?
<--- Score

31. Is the Web Technologies and APIs scope manageable?
<--- Score

32. What are the boundaries of the scope? What is in bounds and what is not? What is the start point? What is the stop point?
<--- Score

33. Have specific policy objectives been defined?
<--- Score

34. Is full participation by members in regularly held team meetings guaranteed?
<--- Score

35. Is the team formed and are team leaders (Coaches and Management Leads) assigned?
<--- Score

36. Will team members perform Web Technologies and APIs work when assigned and in a timely fashion?
<--- Score

37. How did the Web Technologies and APIs manager receive input to the development of a Web Technologies and APIs improvement plan and the estimated completion dates/times of each activity?

<--- Score

38. What customer feedback methods were used to solicit their input?
<--- Score

39. Are roles and responsibilities formally defined?
<--- Score

40. In what way can you redefine the criteria of choice clients have in your category in your favor?
<--- Score

41. Is Web Technologies and APIs required?
<--- Score

42. Are business processes mapped?
<--- Score

43. Is there a Web Technologies and APIs management charter, including business case, problem and goal statements, scope, milestones, roles and responsibilities, communication plan?
<--- Score

44. Are customer(s) identified and segmented according to their different needs and requirements?
<--- Score

45. Is there a completed SIPOC representation, describing the Suppliers, Inputs, Process, Outputs, and Customers?
<--- Score

46. Is data collected and displayed to better understand customer(s) critical needs and

requirements.
<--- Score

47. Have all basic functions of Web Technologies and APIs been defined?
<--- Score

48. When is the estimated completion date?
<--- Score

49. Is the team adequately staffed with the desired cross-functionality? If not, what additional resources are available to the team?
<--- Score

50. What would be the goal or target for a Web Technologies and APIs's improvement team?
<--- Score

51. What are the compelling business reasons for embarking on Web Technologies and APIs?
<--- Score

52. How is the team tracking and documenting its work?
<--- Score

53. Are there any constraints known that bear on the ability to perform Web Technologies and APIs work? How is the team addressing them?
<--- Score

54. What are the record-keeping requirements of Web Technologies and APIs activities?
<--- Score

55. What are the dynamics of the communication plan?
<--- Score

56. Is the improvement team aware of the different versions of a process: what they think it is vs. what it actually is vs. what it should be vs. what it could be?
<--- Score

57. Are team charters developed?
<--- Score

58. What baselines are required to be defined and managed?
<--- Score

59. Has anyone else (internal or external to the organization) attempted to solve this problem or a similar one before? If so, what knowledge can be leveraged from these previous efforts?
<--- Score

60. Who are the Web Technologies and APIs improvement team members, including Management Leads and Coaches?
<--- Score

61. Is the team equipped with available and reliable resources?
<--- Score

62. Has/have the customer(s) been identified?
<--- Score

63. When was the Web Technologies and APIs start date?

<--- Score

64. Is the team sponsored by a champion or business leader?
<--- Score

65. Are required metrics defined, what are they?
<--- Score

66. Who defines (or who defined) the rules and roles?
<--- Score

67. How would you define Web Technologies and APIs leadership?
<--- Score

68. How will the Web Technologies and APIs team and the organization measure complete success of Web Technologies and APIs?
<--- Score

69. Is a fully trained team formed, supported, and committed to work on the Web Technologies and APIs improvements?
<--- Score

70. Are accountability and ownership for Web Technologies and APIs clearly defined?
<--- Score

71. When are meeting minutes sent out? Who is on the distribution list?
<--- Score

72. Have all of the relationships been defined properly?

<--- Score

73. What critical content must be communicated –
who, what, when, where, and how?
<--- Score

74. Has everyone on the team, including the team
leaders, been properly trained?
<--- Score

75. How often are the team meetings?
<--- Score

76. Has the direction changed at all during the course
of Web Technologies and APIs? If so, when did it
change and why?
<--- Score

77. Has the Web Technologies and APIs work been
fairly and/or equitably divided and delegated among
team members who are qualified and capable to
perform the work? Has everyone contributed?
<--- Score

78. How and when will the baselines be defined?
<--- Score

79. How does the Web Technologies and APIs
manager ensure against scope creep?
<--- Score

80. Do the problem and goal statements meet the
SMART criteria (specific, measurable, attainable,
relevant, and time-bound)?
<--- Score

81. In what way can you redefine the criteria of choice in your category in your favor?
<--- Score

82. What constraints exist that might impact the team?
<--- Score

83. Are different versions of process maps needed to account for the different types of inputs?
<--- Score

84. How was the 'as is' process map developed, reviewed, verified and validated?
<--- Score

85. Is there regularly 100% attendance at the team meetings? If not, have appointed substitutes attended to preserve cross-functionality and full representation?
<--- Score

86. Does the team have regular meetings?
<--- Score

Add up total points for this section:
_ _ _ _ _ = Total points for this section

Divided by: _ _ _ _ _ _ (number of statements answered) = _ _ _ _ _ _
Average score for this section

Transfer your score to the Web Technologies and APIs Index at the beginning of the Self-Assessment.

CRITERION #3: MEASURE:

INTENT: Gather the correct data.
Measure the current performance and
evolution of the situation.

In my belief, the answer to this
question is clearly defined:

5 Strongly Agree

4 Agree

3 Neutral

2 Disagree

1 Strongly Disagree

1. How do you identify and analyze stakeholders and
their interests?
<--- Score

2. How frequently do you track Web Technologies and
APIs measures?
<--- Score

3. How do you stay flexible and focused to recognize

35

larger Web Technologies and APIs results?
<--- Score

4. How will your organization measure success?
<--- Score

5. How do you control the overall costs of your work processes?
<--- Score

6. What do you measure and why?
<--- Score

7. Is there a Performance Baseline?
<--- Score

8. Are the measurements objective?
<--- Score

9. Why do the measurements/indicators matter?
<--- Score

10. What are the key input variables? What are the key process variables? What are the key output variables?
<--- Score

11. Have changes been properly/adequately analyzed for effect?
<--- Score

12. Are high impact defects defined and identified in the business process?
<--- Score

13. What is measured?
<--- Score

14. Have the types of risks that may impact Web Technologies and APIs been identified and analyzed?
<--- Score

15. Who participated in the data collection for measurements?
<--- Score

16. How will effects be measured?
<--- Score

17. Who should receive measurement reports?
<--- Score

18. Is the solution cost-effective?
<--- Score

19. Can you do Web Technologies and APIs without complex (expensive) analysis?
<--- Score

20. Do you effectively measure and reward individual and team performance?
<--- Score

21. How can you measure Web Technologies and APIs in a systematic way?
<--- Score

22. How do you aggregate measures across priorities?
<--- Score

23. Does Web Technologies and APIs analysis show the relationships among important Web Technologies and APIs factors?

<--- Score

24. The approach of traditional Web Technologies and APIs works for detail complexity but is focused on a systematic approach rather than an understanding of the nature of systems themselves, what approach will permit your organization to deal with the kind of unpredictable emergent behaviors that dynamic complexity can introduce?
<--- Score

25. Can you measure the return on analysis?
<--- Score

26. Does the Web Technologies and APIs task fit the client's priorities?
<--- Score

27. Have you found any 'ground fruit' or 'low-hanging fruit' for immediate remedies to the gap in performance?
<--- Score

28. Do you aggressively reward and promote the people who have the biggest impact on creating excellent Web Technologies and APIs services/products?
<--- Score

29. Do staff have the necessary skills to collect, analyze, and report data?
<--- Score

30. How will measures be used to manage and adapt?
<--- Score

31. Are losses documented, analyzed, and remedial processes developed to prevent future losses?
<--- Score

32. What methods are feasible and acceptable to estimate the impact of reforms?
<--- Score

33. What are the types and number of measures to use?
<--- Score

34. Was a data collection plan established?
<--- Score

35. What relevant entities could be measured?
<--- Score

36. Are you taking your company in the direction of better and revenue or cheaper and cost?
<--- Score

37. How do you measure lifecycle phases?
<--- Score

38. How are measurements made?
<--- Score

39. What is measured? Why?
<--- Score

40. Which measures and indicators matter?
<--- Score

41. Is a solid data collection plan established that includes measurement systems analysis?

<--- Score

42. Are missed Web Technologies and APIs opportunities costing your organization money?
<--- Score

43. Does your organization systematically track and analyze outcomes related for accountability and quality improvement?
<--- Score

44. What are the costs of reform?
<--- Score

45. How do your measurements capture actionable Web Technologies and APIs information for use in exceeding your customers expectations and securing your customers engagement?
<--- Score

46. What is an unallowable cost?
<--- Score

47. How do you measure success?
<--- Score

48. How do you know that any Web Technologies and APIs analysis is complete and comprehensive?
<--- Score

49. What are your key Web Technologies and APIs indicators that you will measure, analyze and track?
<--- Score

50. What particular quality tools did the team find helpful in establishing measurements?

<--- Score

51. What is the total cost related to deploying Web Technologies and APIs, including any consulting or professional services?
<--- Score

52. What measurements are being captured?
<--- Score

53. Which stakeholder characteristics are analyzed?
<--- Score

54. How will you measure your Web Technologies and APIs effectiveness?
<--- Score

55. Does Web Technologies and APIs systematically track and analyze outcomes for accountability and quality improvement?
<--- Score

56. Is Process Variation Displayed/Communicated?
<--- Score

57. Is data collected on key measures that were identified?
<--- Score

58. What are your key Web Technologies and APIs organizational performance measures, including key short and longer-term financial measures?
<--- Score

59. What charts has the team used to display the components of variation in the process?

<--- Score

60. How will success or failure be measured?
<--- Score

61. Are key measures identified and agreed upon?
<--- Score

62. What data was collected (past, present, future/ongoing)?
<--- Score

63. What are your customers expectations and measures?
<--- Score

64. Are there measurements based on task performance?
<--- Score

65. What measurements are possible, practicable and meaningful?
<--- Score

66. How large is the gap between current performance and the customer-specified (goal) performance?
<--- Score

67. Where is it measured?
<--- Score

68. Have the concerns of stakeholders to help identify and define potential barriers been obtained and analyzed?
<--- Score

69. How do you focus on what is right -not who is right?
<--- Score

70. How is progress measured?
<--- Score

71. How do you do risk analysis of rare, cascading, catastrophic events?
<--- Score

72. Are the units of measure consistent?
<--- Score

73. Are there any easy-to-implement alternatives to Web Technologies and APIs? Sometimes other solutions are available that do not require the cost implications of a full-blown project?
<--- Score

74. What potential environmental factors impact the Web Technologies and APIs effort?
<--- Score

75. Why do you expend time and effort to implement measurement, for whom?
<--- Score

76. What is the right balance of time and resources between investigation, analysis, and discussion and dissemination?
<--- Score

77. Is data collection planned and executed?
<--- Score

78. What are the agreed upon definitions of the high impact areas, defect(s), unit(s), and opportunities that will figure into the process capability metrics?
<--- Score

79. Will Web Technologies and APIs have an impact on current business continuity, disaster recovery processes and/or infrastructure?
<--- Score

80. Among the Web Technologies and APIs product and service cost to be estimated, which is considered hardest to estimate?
<--- Score

81. What evidence is there and what is measured?
<--- Score

82. What has the team done to assure the stability and accuracy of the measurement process?
<--- Score

83. How will you measure success?
<--- Score

84. How to measure variability?
<--- Score

85. How is the value delivered by Web Technologies and APIs being measured?
<--- Score

86. Is key measure data collection planned and executed, process variation displayed and communicated and performance baselined?

<--- Score

87. What are the uncertainties surrounding estimates of impact?
<--- Score

88. What key measures identified indicate the performance of the business process?
<--- Score

89. Is long term and short term variability accounted for?
<--- Score

90. Are process variation components displayed/ communicated using suitable charts, graphs, plots?
<--- Score

91. Have all non-recommended alternatives been analyzed in sufficient detail?
<--- Score

92. Is it possible to estimate the impact of unanticipated complexity such as wrong or failed assumptions, feedback, etc. on proposed reforms?
<--- Score

93. How frequently do you track measures?
<--- Score

94. How are you going to measure success?
<--- Score

95. How can you measure the performance?
<--- Score

96. How is performance measured?
<--- Score

97. Does Web Technologies and APIs analysis isolate the fundamental causes of problems?
<--- Score

Add up total points for this section:
_____ = Total points for this section

Divided by: _____ (number of statements answered) = _____
Average score for this section

Transfer your score to the Web Technologies and APIs Index at the beginning of the Self-Assessment.

CRITERION #4: ANALYZE:

INTENT: Analyze causes, assumptions and hypotheses.

In my belief, the answer to this question is clearly defined:

5 Strongly Agree

4 Agree

3 Neutral

2 Disagree

1 Strongly Disagree

1. Did any value-added analysis or 'lean thinking' take place to identify some of the gaps shown on the 'as is' process map?
<--- Score

2. Have any additional benefits been identified that will result from closing all or most of the gaps?
<--- Score

3. How is the way you as the leader think and process

information affecting your organizational culture?
<--- Score

4. What is the cost of poor quality as supported by the team's analysis?
<--- Score

5. Are gaps between current performance and the goal performance identified?
<--- Score

6. What are the revised rough estimates of the financial savings/opportunity for Web Technologies and APIs improvements?
<--- Score

7. What are your current levels and trends in key measures or indicators of Web Technologies and APIs product and process performance that are important to and directly serve your customers? How do these results compare with the performance of your competitors and other organizations with similar offerings?
<--- Score

8. Is the suppliers process defined and controlled?
<--- Score

9. What process should you select for improvement?
<--- Score

10. Was a cause-and-effect diagram used to explore the different types of causes (or sources of variation)?
<--- Score

11. What controls do you have in place to protect

data?
<--- Score

12. What were the financial benefits resulting from any 'ground fruit or low-hanging fruit' (quick fixes)?
<--- Score

13. Is the gap/opportunity displayed and communicated in financial terms?
<--- Score

14. How often will data be collected for measures?
<--- Score

15. Did any additional data need to be collected?
<--- Score

16. What are the best opportunities for value improvement?
<--- Score

17. How do you promote understanding that opportunity for improvement is not criticism of the status quo, or the people who created the status quo?
<--- Score

18. Identify an operational issue in your organization. for example, could a particular task be done more quickly or more efficiently by Web Technologies and APIs?
<--- Score

19. Do your employees have the opportunity to do what they do best everyday?
<--- Score

20. What does the data say about the performance of the business process?
<--- Score

21. Were any designed experiments used to generate additional insight into the data analysis?
<--- Score

22. Do several people in different organizational units assist with the Web Technologies and APIs process?
<--- Score

23. What did the team gain from developing a sub-process map?
<--- Score

24. Is the Web Technologies and APIs process severely broken such that a re-design is necessary?
<--- Score

25. How do you identify specific Web Technologies and APIs investment opportunities and emerging trends?
<--- Score

26. Was a detailed process map created to amplify critical steps of the 'as is' business process?
<--- Score

27. Is the performance gap determined?
<--- Score

28. How do your work systems and key work processes relate to and capitalize on your core competencies?
<--- Score

29. Record-keeping requirements flow from the records needed as inputs, outputs, controls and for transformation of a Web Technologies and APIs process. Are the records needed as inputs to the Web Technologies and APIs process available?
<--- Score

30. What other jobs or tasks affect the performance of the steps in the Web Technologies and APIs process?
<--- Score

31. What are the disruptive Web Technologies and APIs technologies that enable your organization to radically change your business processes?
<--- Score

32. When conducting a business process reengineering study, what do you look for when trying to identify business processes to change?
<--- Score

33. What tools were used to narrow the list of possible causes?
<--- Score

34. Think about the functions involved in your Web Technologies and APIs project, what processes flow from these functions?
<--- Score

35. What tools were used to generate the list of possible causes?
<--- Score

36. What conclusions were drawn from the team's

data collection and analysis? How did the team reach these conclusions?

<--- Score

37. Can you add value to the current Web Technologies and APIs decision-making process (largely qualitative) by incorporating uncertainty modeling (more quantitative)?

<--- Score

38. What are your current levels and trends in key Web Technologies and APIs measures or indicators of product and process performance that are important to and directly serve your customers?

<--- Score

39. Were there any improvement opportunities identified from the process analysis?

<--- Score

40. An organizationally feasible system request is one that considers the mission, goals and objectives of the organization. Key questions are: is the Web Technologies and APIs solution request practical and will it solve a problem or take advantage of an opportunity to achieve company goals?

<--- Score

41. What are your key performance measures or indicators and in-process measures for the control and improvement of your Web Technologies and APIs processes?

<--- Score

42. Do your leaders quickly bounce back from setbacks?

<--- Score

43. What successful thing are you doing today that may be blinding you to new growth opportunities?
<--- Score

44. What are your best practices for minimizing Web Technologies and APIs project risk, while demonstrating incremental value and quick wins throughout the Web Technologies and APIs project lifecycle?
<--- Score

45. What are your Web Technologies and APIs processes?
<--- Score

46. How do you implement and manage your work processes to ensure that they meet design requirements?
<--- Score

47. A compounding model resolution with available relevant data can often provide insight towards a solution methodology; which Web Technologies and APIs models, tools and techniques are necessary?
<--- Score

48. Do you, as a leader, bounce back quickly from setbacks?
<--- Score

49. Were Pareto charts (or similar) used to portray the 'heavy hitters' (or key sources of variation)?
<--- Score

50. What quality tools were used to get through the analyze phase?
<--- Score

51. Where is the data coming from to measure compliance?
<--- Score

52. How does the organization define, manage, and improve its Web Technologies and APIs processes?
<--- Score

53. How was the detailed process map generated, verified, and validated?
<--- Score

54. How do you measure the operational performance of your key work systems and processes, including productivity, cycle time, and other appropriate measures of process effectiveness, efficiency, and innovation?
<--- Score

55. Have the problem and goal statements been updated to reflect the additional knowledge gained from the analyze phase?
<--- Score

56. How do mission and objectives affect the Web Technologies and APIs processes of your organization?
<--- Score

57. Think about some of the processes you undertake within your organization, which do you own?
<--- Score

58. What were the crucial 'moments of truth' on the process map?
<--- Score

59. How do you use Web Technologies and APIs data and information to support organizational decision making and innovation?
<--- Score

60. What other organizational variables, such as reward systems or communication systems, affect the performance of this Web Technologies and APIs process?
<--- Score

61. Is Data and process analysis, root cause analysis and quantifying the gap/opportunity in place?
<--- Score

Add up total points for this section:
_____ = Total points for this section

Divided by: _____ (number of statements answered) = _____
Average score for this section

Transfer your score to the Web Technologies and APIs Index at the beginning of the Self-Assessment.

CRITERION #5: IMPROVE:

INTENT: Develop a practical solution. Innovate, establish and test the solution and to measure the results.

In my belief, the answer to this question is clearly defined:

5 Strongly Agree

4 Agree

3 Neutral

2 Disagree

1 Strongly Disagree

1. What resources are required for the improvement efforts?
<--- Score

2. Were any criteria developed to assist the team in testing and evaluating potential solutions?
<--- Score

3. Are improved process ('should be') maps modified

based on pilot data and analysis?
<--- Score

4. What lessons, if any, from a pilot were incorporated into the design of the full-scale solution?
<--- Score

5. Is a contingency plan established?
<--- Score

6. Who will be responsible for making the decisions to include or exclude requested changes once Web Technologies and APIs is underway?
<--- Score

7. What went well, what should change, what can improve?
<--- Score

8. Risk factors: what are the characteristics of Web Technologies and APIs that make it risky?
<--- Score

9. What does the 'should be' process map/design look like?
<--- Score

10. What is Web Technologies and APIs's impact on utilizing the best solution(s)?
<--- Score

11. What are your current levels and trends in key measures or indicators of workforce and leader development?
<--- Score

12. Are new and improved process ('should be') maps developed?
<--- Score

13. What should a proof of concept or pilot accomplish?
<--- Score

14. Who controls the risk?
<--- Score

15. Is the implementation plan designed?
<--- Score

16. What tools were used to evaluate the potential solutions?
<--- Score

17. Can the solution be designed and implemented within an acceptable time period?
<--- Score

18. What needs improvement? Why?
<--- Score

19. What were the underlying assumptions on the cost-benefit analysis?
<--- Score

20. How do you improve productivity?
<--- Score

21. How will the organization know that the solution worked?
<--- Score

22. How can you improve Web Technologies and APIs?
<--- Score

23. Risk events: what are the things that could go wrong?
<--- Score

24. Is the measure of success for Web Technologies and APIs understandable to a variety of people?
<--- Score

25. How do you link measurement and risk?
<--- Score

26. Is the optimal solution selected based on testing and analysis?
<--- Score

27. How do you improve Web Technologies and APIs service perception, and satisfaction?
<--- Score

28. In the past few months, what is the smallest change you have made that has had the biggest positive result? What was it about that small change that produced the large return?
<--- Score

29. How did the team generate the list of possible solutions?
<--- Score

30. If you could go back in time five years, what decision would you make differently? What is your best guess as to what decision you're making today you might regret five years from now?

<--- Score

31. Do those selected for the Web Technologies and APIs team have a good general understanding of what Web Technologies and APIs is all about?
<--- Score

32. To what extent does management recognize Web Technologies and APIs as a tool to increase the results?
<--- Score

33. Are the best solutions selected?
<--- Score

34. For decision problems, how do you develop a decision statement?
<--- Score

35. At what point will vulnerability assessments be performed once Web Technologies and APIs is put into production (e.g., ongoing Risk Management after implementation)?
<--- Score

36. What improvements have been achieved?
<--- Score

37. Do you combine technical expertise with business knowledge and Web Technologies and APIs Key topics include lifecycles, development approaches, requirements and how to make a business case?
<--- Score

38. How do you measure improved Web Technologies and APIs service perception, and satisfaction?

<--- Score

39. How do you measure risk?
<--- Score

40. What is the Web Technologies and APIs's sustainability risk?
<--- Score

41. How do you manage and improve your Web Technologies and APIs work systems to deliver customer value and achieve organizational success and sustainability?
<--- Score

42. Is the solution technically practical?
<--- Score

43. What communications are necessary to support the implementation of the solution?
<--- Score

44. Is supporting Web Technologies and APIs documentation required?
<--- Score

45. How can you improve performance?
<--- Score

46. How will you know that you have improved?
<--- Score

47. What is the risk?
<--- Score

48. How do you decide how much to remunerate an

employee?

<--- Score

49. How do the Web Technologies and APIs results compare with the performance of your competitors and other organizations with similar offerings?

<--- Score

50. How does the solution remove the key sources of issues discovered in the analyze phase?

<--- Score

51. What is the team's contingency plan for potential problems occurring in implementation?

<--- Score

52. Who will be responsible for documenting the Web Technologies and APIs requirements in detail?

<--- Score

53. Who controls key decisions that will be made?

<--- Score

54. Is there a high likelihood that any recommendations will achieve their intended results?

<--- Score

55. Describe the design of the pilot and what tests were conducted, if any?

<--- Score

56. What attendant changes will need to be made to ensure that the solution is successful?

<--- Score

57. What error proofing will be done to address some

of the discrepancies observed in the 'as is' process?
<--- Score

58. Are you assessing Web Technologies and APIs and risk?
<--- Score

59. How can skill-level changes improve Web Technologies and APIs?
<--- Score

60. What is the implementation plan?
<--- Score

61. How do you go about comparing Web Technologies and APIs approaches/solutions?
<--- Score

62. What do you want to improve?
<--- Score

63. How will you measure the results?
<--- Score

64. What are the implications of the one critical Web Technologies and APIs decision 10 minutes, 10 months, and 10 years from now?
<--- Score

65. Who will be using the results of the measurement activities?
<--- Score

66. What tools do you use once you have decided on a Web Technologies and APIs strategy and more importantly how do you choose?

<--- Score

67. What to do with the results or outcomes of measurements?
<--- Score

68. Is there a small-scale pilot for proposed improvement(s)? What conclusions were drawn from the outcomes of a pilot?
<--- Score

69. Is a solution implementation plan established, including schedule/work breakdown structure, resources, risk management plan, cost/budget, and control plan?
<--- Score

70. Why improve in the first place?
<--- Score

71. How will you know that a change is an improvement?
<--- Score

72. Are possible solutions generated and tested?
<--- Score

73. Is there a cost/benefit analysis of optimal solution(s)?
<--- Score

74. How do you improve your likelihood of success ?
<--- Score

75. How does the team improve its work?
<--- Score

76. Are there any constraints (technical, political, cultural, or otherwise) that would inhibit certain solutions?
<--- Score

77. What is the magnitude of the improvements?
<--- Score

78. Do you cover the five essential competencies: Communication, Collaboration,Innovation, Adaptability, and Leadership that improve an organization's ability to leverage the new Web Technologies and APIs in a volatile global economy?
<--- Score

79. Was a pilot designed for the proposed solution(s)?
<--- Score

80. How do you measure progress and evaluate training effectiveness?
<--- Score

81. Who are the people involved in developing and implementing Web Technologies and APIs?
<--- Score

82. What tools were most useful during the improve phase?
<--- Score

83. What tools were used to tap into the creativity and encourage 'outside the box' thinking?
<--- Score

84. What can you do to improve?

<--- Score

85. Explorations of the frontiers of Web Technologies and APIs will help you build influence, improve Web Technologies and APIs, optimize decision making, and sustain change, what is your approach?
<--- Score

86. How will the team or the process owner(s) monitor the implementation plan to see that it is working as intended?
<--- Score

87. For estimation problems, how do you develop an estimation statement?
<--- Score

88. How do you keep improving Web Technologies and APIs?
<--- Score

89. How significant is the improvement in the eyes of the end user?
<--- Score

90. What actually has to improve and by how much?
<--- Score

91. Is pilot data collected and analyzed?
<--- Score

92. Does the goal represent a desired result that can be measured?
<--- Score

93. How will you know when its improved?

<--- Score

Add up total points for this section:
_ _ _ _ _ = Total points for this section

Divided by: _ _ _ _ _ _ (number of
statements answered) = _ _ _ _ _ _
Average score for this section

Transfer your score to the Web
Technologies and APIs Index at the
beginning of the Self-Assessment.

CRITERION #6: CONTROL:

INTENT: Implement the practical solution. Maintain the performance and correct possible complications.

In my belief, the answer to this question is clearly defined:

5 Strongly Agree

4 Agree

3 Neutral

2 Disagree

1 Strongly Disagree

1. Does Web Technologies and APIs appropriately measure and monitor risk?
<--- Score

2. Against what alternative is success being measured?
<--- Score

3. Is there a transfer of ownership and knowledge

to process owner and process team tasked with the responsibilities.
<--- Score

4. How likely is the current Web Technologies and APIs plan to come in on schedule or on budget?
<--- Score

5. Is knowledge gained on process shared and institutionalized?
<--- Score

6. Are the planned controls in place?
<--- Score

7. Who has control over resources?
<--- Score

8. You may have created your quality measures at a time when you lacked resources, technology wasn't up to the required standard, or low service levels were the industry norm. Have those circumstances changed?
<--- Score

9. Is there a recommended audit plan for routine surveillance inspections of Web Technologies and APIs's gains?
<--- Score

10. Are controls in place and consistently applied?
<--- Score

11. Who is the Web Technologies and APIs process owner?
<--- Score

12. How do your controls stack up?
<--- Score

13. What other areas of the organization might benefit from the Web Technologies and APIs team's improvements, knowledge, and learning?
<--- Score

14. How will the day-to-day responsibilities for monitoring and continual improvement be transferred from the improvement team to the process owner?
<--- Score

15. In the case of a Web Technologies and APIs project, the criteria for the audit derive from implementation objectives. an audit of a Web Technologies and APIs project involves assessing whether the recommendations outlined for implementation have been met. Can you track that any Web Technologies and APIs project is implemented as planned, and is it working?
<--- Score

16. How will the process owner and team be able to hold the gains?
<--- Score

17. Do the decisions you make today help people and the planet tomorrow?
<--- Score

18. How can you best use all of your knowledge repositories to enhance learning and sharing?
<--- Score

19. What is the recommended frequency of auditing?
<--- Score

20. Do you monitor the Web Technologies and APIs decisions made and fine tune them as they evolve?
<--- Score

21. Have new or revised work instructions resulted?
<--- Score

22. What should you measure to verify efficiency gains?
<--- Score

23. Does job training on the documented procedures need to be part of the process team's education and training?
<--- Score

24. Who sets the Web Technologies and APIs standards?
<--- Score

25. How do controls support value?
<--- Score

26. Implementation Planning- is a pilot needed to test the changes before a full roll out occurs?
<--- Score

27. Are the planned controls working?
<--- Score

28. Does the Web Technologies and APIs performance meet the customer's requirements?

<--- Score

29. Are operating procedures consistent?
<--- Score

30. How might the organization capture best practices and lessons learned so as to leverage improvements across the business?
<--- Score

31. Is there documentation that will support the successful operation of the improvement?
<--- Score

32. Is there a documented and implemented monitoring plan?
<--- Score

33. Are new process steps, standards, and documentation ingrained into normal operations?
<--- Score

34. How will new or emerging customer needs/ requirements be checked/communicated to orient the process toward meeting the new specifications and continually reducing variation?
<--- Score

35. Is there a standardized process?
<--- Score

36. How do you encourage people to take control and responsibility?
<--- Score

37. Is new knowledge gained imbedded in the

response plan?
<--- Score

38. What are your results for key measures or indicators of the accomplishment of your Web Technologies and APIs strategy and action plans, including building and strengthening core competencies?
<--- Score

39. What quality tools were useful in the control phase?
<--- Score

40. What do you measure to verify effectiveness gains?
<--- Score

41. Where do ideas that reach policy makers and planners as proposals for Web Technologies and APIs strengthening and reform actually originate?
<--- Score

42. What do you stand for--and what are you against?
<--- Score

43. How will the process owner verify improvement in present and future sigma levels, process capabilities?
<--- Score

44. Is a response plan in place for when the input, process, or output measures indicate an 'out-of-control' condition?
<--- Score

45. Does a troubleshooting guide exist or is it needed?

<--- Score

46. What other systems, operations, processes, and infrastructures (hiring practices, staffing, training, incentives/rewards, metrics/dashboards/scorecards, etc.) need updates, additions, changes, or deletions in order to facilitate knowledge transfer and improvements?
<--- Score

47. What is the best design framework for Web Technologies and APIs organization now that, in a post industrial-age if the top-down, command and control model is no longer relevant?
<--- Score

48. What are the critical parameters to watch?
<--- Score

49. What are the known security controls?
<--- Score

50. Are pertinent alerts monitored, analyzed and distributed to appropriate personnel?
<--- Score

51. Are you measuring, monitoring and predicting Web Technologies and APIs activities to optimize operations and profitability, and enhancing outcomes?
<--- Score

52. Is there a Web Technologies and APIs Communication plan covering who needs to get what information when?
<--- Score

53. Is reporting being used or needed?
<--- Score

54. What can you control?
<--- Score

55. How do you select, collect, align, and integrate Web Technologies and APIs data and information for tracking daily operations and overall organizational performance, including progress relative to strategic objectives and action plans?
<--- Score

56. Is there a control plan in place for sustaining improvements (short and long-term)?
<--- Score

57. Who will be in control?
<--- Score

58. What should the next improvement project be that is related to Web Technologies and APIs?
<--- Score

59. How is change control managed?
<--- Score

60. How will report readings be checked to effectively monitor performance?
<--- Score

61. Are there documented procedures?
<--- Score

62. Are suggested corrective/restorative actions

indicated on the response plan for known causes to problems that might surface?

<--- Score

63. What are the key elements of your Web Technologies and APIs performance improvement system, including your evaluation, organizational learning, and innovation processes?

<--- Score

64. Has the improved process and its steps been standardized?

<--- Score

65. Are documented procedures clear and easy to follow for the operators?

<--- Score

66. Who controls critical resources?

<--- Score

67. Is a response plan established and deployed?

<--- Score

68. What is your theory of human motivation, and how does your compensation plan fit with that view?

<--- Score

69. Does the response plan contain a definite closed loop continual improvement scheme (e.g., plan-do-check-act)?

<--- Score

70. What is the control/monitoring plan?

<--- Score

71. Do the Web Technologies and APIs decisions you make today help people and the planet tomorrow?
<--- Score

72. How do you establish and deploy modified action plans if circumstances require a shift in plans and rapid execution of new plans?
<--- Score

73. How will input, process, and output variables be checked to detect for sub-optimal conditions?
<--- Score

74. What are you attempting to measure/monitor?
<--- Score

75. Will existing staff require re-training, for example, to learn new business processes?
<--- Score

76. What key inputs and outputs are being measured on an ongoing basis?
<--- Score

77. Will any special training be provided for results interpretation?
<--- Score

78. Do you monitor the effectiveness of your Web Technologies and APIs activities?
<--- Score

Add up total points for this section:
_ _ _ _ _ = Total points for this section

Divided by: _ _ _ _ _ _ (number of

statements answered) = _____
Average score for this section

Transfer your score to the Web
Technologies and APIs Index at the
beginning of the Self-Assessment.

CRITERION #7: SUSTAIN:

INTENT: Retain the benefits.

In my belief, the answer to this
question is clearly defined:

5 Strongly Agree

4 Agree

3 Neutral

2 Disagree

1 Strongly Disagree

1. What role does communication play in the success
or failure of a Web Technologies and APIs project?
<--- Score

2. If you had to leave your organization for a year
and the only communication you could have with
employees/colleagues was a single paragraph, what
would you write?
<--- Score

3. How much does Web Technologies and APIs help?

<--- Score

4. How do you keep records, of what?
<--- Score

5. How is business? Why?
<--- Score

6. How do you manage Web Technologies and APIs Knowledge Management (KM)?
<--- Score

7. Why is it important to have senior management support for a Web Technologies and APIs project?
<--- Score

8. Are assumptions made in Web Technologies and APIs stated explicitly?
<--- Score

9. What is the source of the strategies for Web Technologies and APIs strengthening and reform?
<--- Score

10. What will be the consequences to the stakeholder (financial, reputation etc) if Web Technologies and APIs does not go ahead or fails to deliver the objectives?
<--- Score

11. When information truly is ubiquitous, when reach and connectivity are completely global, when computing resources are infinite, and when a whole new set of impossibilities are not only possible, but happening, what will that do to your business?
<--- Score

12. How can you become more high-tech but still be high touch?
<--- Score

13. Which models, tools and techniques are necessary?
<--- Score

14. What are you trying to prove to yourself, and how might it be hijacking your life and business success?
<--- Score

15. What counts that you are not counting?
<--- Score

16. What would you recommend your friend do if he/she were facing this dilemma?
<--- Score

17. Who is responsible for errors?
<--- Score

18. How will you insure seamless interoperability of Web Technologies and APIs moving forward?
<--- Score

19. Who have you, as a company, historically been when you've been at your best?
<--- Score

20. What is an unauthorized commitment?
<--- Score

21. At what moment would you think; Will I get fired?
<--- Score

22. If no one would ever find out about your accomplishments, how would you lead differently?
<--- Score

23. What may be the consequences for the performance of an organization if all stakeholders are not consulted regarding Web Technologies and APIs?
<--- Score

24. Whom among your colleagues do you trust, and for what?
<--- Score

25. Political -is anyone trying to undermine this project?
<--- Score

26. How likely is it that a customer would recommend your company to a friend or colleague?
<--- Score

27. What did you miss in the interview for the worst hire you ever made?
<--- Score

28. Can the schedule be done in the given time?
<--- Score

29. What are the rules and assumptions your industry operates under? What if the opposite were true?
<--- Score

30. In a project to restructure Web Technologies and APIs outcomes, which stakeholders would you involve?

<--- Score

31. How do you determine the key elements
that affect Web Technologies and APIs workforce
satisfaction, how are these elements determined for
different workforce groups and segments?
<--- Score

32. How do you stay inspired?
<--- Score

33. What are specific Web Technologies and APIs rules
to follow?
<--- Score

34. Who, on the executive team or the board, has
spoken to a customer recently?
<--- Score

35. Who is responsible for Web Technologies and
APIs?
<--- Score

36. Whose voice (department, ethnic group, women,
older workers, etc) might you have missed hearing
from in your company, and how might you amplify
this voice to create positive momentum for your
business?
<--- Score

37. What happens when a new employee joins the
organization?
<--- Score

38. What are the gaps in your knowledge and
experience?

<--- Score

39. Have benefits been optimized with all key stakeholders?
<--- Score

40. What does your signature ensure?
<--- Score

41. Where can you break convention?
<--- Score

42. To whom do you add value?
<--- Score

43. If you were responsible for initiating and implementing major changes in your organization, what steps might you take to ensure acceptance of those changes?
<--- Score

44. Do you know what you are doing? And who do you call if you don't?
<--- Score

45. How do you go about securing Web Technologies and APIs?
<--- Score

46. What was the last experiment you ran?
<--- Score

47. What one word do you want to own in the minds of your customers, employees, and partners?
<--- Score

48. Are new benefits received and understood?
<--- Score

49. What is the range of capabilities?
<--- Score

50. Have new benefits been realized?
<--- Score

51. What sources do you use to gather information for a Web Technologies and APIs study?
<--- Score

52. Why not do Web Technologies and APIs?
<--- Score

53. What are strategies for increasing support and reducing opposition?
<--- Score

54. What is a feasible sequencing of reform initiatives over time?
<--- Score

55. How do you cross-sell and up-sell your Web Technologies and APIs success?
<--- Score

56. In retrospect, of the projects that you pulled the plug on, what percent do you wish had been allowed to keep going, and what percent do you wish had ended earlier?
<--- Score

57. What is the estimated value of the project?
<--- Score

58. How do you accomplish your long range Web Technologies and APIs goals?
<--- Score

59. Did your employees make progress today?
<--- Score

60. Are the assumptions believable and achievable?
<--- Score

61. What happens if you do not have enough funding?
<--- Score

62. Who will provide the final approval of Web Technologies and APIs deliverables?
<--- Score

63. What is your competitive advantage?
<--- Score

64. How do you track customer value, profitability or financial return, organizational success, and sustainability?
<--- Score

65. What potential megatrends could make your business model obsolete?
<--- Score

66. What threat is Web Technologies and APIs addressing?
<--- Score

67. Are you satisfied with your current role? If not,

what is missing from it?
<--- Score

68. Do you see more potential in people than they do in themselves?
<--- Score

69. Are you paying enough attention to the partners your company depends on to succeed?
<--- Score

70. Why should you adopt a Web Technologies and APIs framework?
<--- Score

71. How do you make it meaningful in connecting Web Technologies and APIs with what users do day-to-day?
<--- Score

72. What is the craziest thing you can do?
<--- Score

73. What will drive Web Technologies and APIs change?
<--- Score

74. Who uses your product in ways you never expected?
<--- Score

75. What have you done to protect your business from competitive encroachment?
<--- Score

76. What information is critical to your organization

that your executives are ignoring?

<--- Score

77. How do you ensure that implementations of Web Technologies and APIs products are done in a way that ensures safety?

<--- Score

78. Who do you want your customers to become?

<--- Score

79. What trophy do you want on your mantle?

<--- Score

80. What are the long-term Web Technologies and APIs goals?

<--- Score

81. Who is on the team?

<--- Score

82. Is there any reason to believe the opposite of my current belief?

<--- Score

83. What is it like to work for you?

<--- Score

84. How do you govern and fulfill your societal responsibilities?

<--- Score

85. Why is Web Technologies and APIs important for you now?

<--- Score

86. Who are four people whose careers you have enhanced?
<--- Score

87. What management system can you use to leverage the Web Technologies and APIs experience, ideas, and concerns of the people closest to the work to be done?
<--- Score

88. If there were zero limitations, what would you do differently?
<--- Score

89. What current systems have to be understood and/or changed?
<--- Score

90. What happens at your organization when people fail?
<--- Score

91. How do you proactively clarify deliverables and Web Technologies and APIs quality expectations?
<--- Score

92. How can you incorporate support to ensure safe and effective use of Web Technologies and APIs into the services that you provide?
<--- Score

93. How will you know that the Web Technologies and APIs project has been successful?
<--- Score

94. How will you motivate the stakeholders with the

least vested interest?
<--- Score

95. Do you have the right capabilities and capacities?
<--- Score

96. How do you foster innovation?
<--- Score

97. How do you foster the skills, knowledge, talents, attributes, and characteristics you want to have?
<--- Score

98. Who do you think the world wants your organization to be?
<--- Score

99. What business benefits will Web Technologies and APIs goals deliver if achieved?
<--- Score

100. Is your strategy driving your strategy? Or is the way in which you allocate resources driving your strategy?
<--- Score

101. How do you know if you are successful?
<--- Score

102. Are you relevant? Will you be relevant five years from now? Ten?
<--- Score

103. How are you doing compared to your industry?
<--- Score

104. Will it be accepted by users?
<--- Score

105. Think of your Web Technologies and APIs project, what are the main functions?
<--- Score

106. Who are the key stakeholders?
<--- Score

107. What is something you believe that nearly no one agrees with you on?
<--- Score

108. Which Web Technologies and APIs goals are the most important?
<--- Score

109. Who is the main stakeholder, with ultimate responsibility for driving Web Technologies and APIs forward?
<--- Score

110. How long will it take to change?
<--- Score

111. What do we do when new problems arise?
<--- Score

112. Are you making progress, and are you making progress as Web Technologies and APIs leaders?
<--- Score

113. Who will be responsible for deciding whether Web Technologies and APIs goes ahead or not after the initial investigations?

<--- Score

114. Is the Web Technologies and APIs organization completing tasks effectively and efficiently?
<--- Score

115. Would you rather sell to knowledgeable and informed customers or to uninformed customers?
<--- Score

116. Are you / should you be revolutionary or evolutionary?
<--- Score

117. What stupid rule would you most like to kill?
<--- Score

118. How important is Web Technologies and APIs to the user organizations mission?
<--- Score

119. Do you think you know, or do you know you know ?
<--- Score

120. Do you have enough freaky customers in your portfolio pushing you to the limit day in and day out?
<--- Score

121. Operational - will it work?
<--- Score

122. Do you have past Web Technologies and APIs successes?
<--- Score

123. What is your Web Technologies and APIs strategy?
<--- Score

124. What is your question? Why?
<--- Score

125. If your company went out of business tomorrow, would anyone who doesn't get a paycheck here care?
<--- Score

126. Why should people listen to you?
<--- Score

127. What are the potential basics of Web Technologies and APIs fraud?
<--- Score

128. How do you provide a safe environment -physically and emotionally?
<--- Score

129. Who will manage the integration of tools?
<--- Score

130. What are the short and long-term Web Technologies and APIs goals?
<--- Score

131. What would have to be true for the option on the table to be the best possible choice?
<--- Score

132. If you got fired and a new hire took your place, what would she do different?
<--- Score

133. How do you create buy-in?
<--- Score

134. Is there any existing Web Technologies and APIs governance structure?
<--- Score

135. What are the barriers to increased Web Technologies and APIs production?
<--- Score

136. How do senior leaders actions reflect a commitment to the organizations Web Technologies and APIs values?
<--- Score

137. How can you negotiate Web Technologies and APIs successfully with a stubborn boss, an irate client, or a deceitful coworker?
<--- Score

138. How do you keep the momentum going?
<--- Score

139. What are your most important goals for the strategic Web Technologies and APIs objectives?
<--- Score

140. Will there be any necessary staff changes (redundancies or new hires)?
<--- Score

141. Ask yourself: how would you do this work if you only had one staff member to do it?
<--- Score

142. How do you lead with Web Technologies and APIs in mind?
<--- Score

143. What are the top 3 things at the forefront of your Web Technologies and APIs agendas for the next 3 years?
<--- Score

144. If you weren't already in this business, would you enter it today? And if not, what are you going to do about it?
<--- Score

145. Is maximizing Web Technologies and APIs protection the same as minimizing Web Technologies and APIs loss?
<--- Score

146. Is it economical; do you have the time and money?
<--- Score

147. How do you listen to customers to obtain actionable information?
<--- Score

148. Who do we want your customers to become?
<--- Score

149. What is your formula for success in Web Technologies and APIs ?
<--- Score

150. What should you stop doing?

<--- Score

151. Do Web Technologies and APIs rules make a reasonable demand on a users capabilities?
<--- Score

152. What kind of crime could a potential new hire have committed that would not only not disqualify him/her from being hired by your organization, but would actually indicate that he/she might be a particularly good fit?
<--- Score

153. Do you say no to customers for no reason?
<--- Score

154. Marketing budgets are tighter, consumers are more skeptical, and social media has changed forever the way we talk about Web Technologies and APIs. How do you gain traction?
<--- Score

155. Which functions and people interact with the supplier and or customer?
<--- Score

156. What are the essentials of internal Web Technologies and APIs management?
<--- Score

157. How do you maintain Web Technologies and APIs's Integrity?
<--- Score

158. How can you become the company that would put you out of business?

<--- Score

159. How will you ensure you get what you expected?
<--- Score

160. Has implementation been effective in reaching specified objectives so far?
<--- Score

161. If your customer were your grandmother, would you tell her to buy what you're selling?
<--- Score

162. Are there any disadvantages to implementing Web Technologies and APIs? There might be some that are less obvious?
<--- Score

163. What are the success criteria that will indicate that Web Technologies and APIs objectives have been met and the benefits delivered?
<--- Score

164. If you had to rebuild your organization without any traditional competitive advantages (i.e., no killer a technology, promising research, innovative product/ service delivery model, etc.), how would your people have to approach their work and collaborate together in order to create the necessary conditions for success?
<--- Score

165. What is effective Web Technologies and APIs?
<--- Score

166. What are you challenging?

<--- Score

167. Why do and why don't your customers like your organization?
<--- Score

168. What is the purpose of Web Technologies and APIs in relation to the mission?
<--- Score

169. Are you failing differently each time?
<--- Score

170. How do you engage the workforce, in addition to satisfying them?
<--- Score

171. Who else should you help?
<--- Score

172. What new services of functionality will be implemented next with Web Technologies and APIs ?
<--- Score

173. How much contingency will be available in the budget?
<--- Score

174. What are the business goals Web Technologies and APIs is aiming to achieve?
<--- Score

175. If you do not follow, then how to lead?
<--- Score

176. Is Web Technologies and APIs realistic, or are you

setting yourself up for failure?
<--- Score

177. How do customers see your organization?
<--- Score

178. Instead of going to current contacts for new ideas, what if you reconnected with dormant contacts--the people you used to know? If you were going reactivate a dormant tie, who would it be?
<--- Score

179. What trouble can you get into?
<--- Score

180. How do senior leaders deploy your organizations vision and values through your leadership system, to the workforce, to key suppliers and partners, and to customers and other stakeholders, as appropriate?
<--- Score

181. Among your stronger employees, how many see themselves at the company in three years? How many would leave for a 10 percent raise from another company?
<--- Score

182. What is the overall business strategy?
<--- Score

183. Do you have an implicit bias for capital investments over people investments?
<--- Score

184. What Web Technologies and APIs skills are most important?

<--- Score

185. How do you assess the Web Technologies and APIs pitfalls that are inherent in implementing it?
<--- Score

186. Is Web Technologies and APIs dependent on the successful delivery of a current project?
<--- Score

187. What are current Web Technologies and APIs paradigms?
<--- Score

188. Can you maintain your growth without detracting from the factors that have contributed to your success?
<--- Score

189. What are the challenges?
<--- Score

190. How does Web Technologies and APIs integrate with other business initiatives?
<--- Score

191. Do you have the right people on the bus?
<--- Score

192. How do you deal with Web Technologies and APIs changes?
<--- Score

193. Which individuals, teams or departments will be involved in Web Technologies and APIs?
<--- Score

194. In the past year, what have you done (or could you have done) to increase the accurate perception of your company/brand as ethical and honest?
<--- Score

195. What are the usability implications of Web Technologies and APIs actions?
<--- Score

196. Is a Web Technologies and APIs team work effort in place?
<--- Score

197. Who is responsible for ensuring appropriate resources (time, people and money) are allocated to Web Technologies and APIs?
<--- Score

198. Who will determine interim and final deadlines?
<--- Score

199. What is the kind of project structure that would be appropriate for your Web Technologies and APIs project, should it be formal and complex, or can it be less formal and relatively simple?
<--- Score

200. Is the impact that Web Technologies and APIs has shown?
<--- Score

201. Are the criteria for selecting recommendations stated?
<--- Score

202. What knowledge, skills and characteristics mark a good Web Technologies and APIs project manager?
<--- Score

203. What are internal and external Web Technologies and APIs relations?
<--- Score

204. Are you changing as fast as the world around you?
<--- Score

205. What is the funding source for this project?
<--- Score

206. What are the key enablers to make this Web Technologies and APIs move?
<--- Score

207. Are you using a design thinking approach and integrating Innovation, Web Technologies and APIs Experience, and Brand Value?
<--- Score

208. Were lessons learned captured and communicated?
<--- Score

209. What is your BATNA (best alternative to a negotiated agreement)?
<--- Score

Add up total points for this section:
_ _ _ _ _ = Total points for this section

Divided by: _ _ _ _ _ _ (number of

statements answered) = _____
Average score for this section

Transfer your score to the Web
Technologies and APIs Index at the
beginning of the Self-Assessment.

Web Technologies and APIs and Managing Projects, Criteria for Project Managers:

1.0 Initiating Process Group: Web Technologies and APIs

1. Does the Web Technologies and APIs project team have enough people to execute the Web Technologies and APIs project plan?

2. Have you evaluated the teams performance and asked for feedback?

3. For technology Web Technologies and APIs projects only: Are all production support stakeholders (Business unit, technical support, & user) prepared for implementation with appropriate contingency plans?

4. Are the Web Technologies and APIs project team and stakeholders meeting regularly and using a meeting agenda and taking notes to accurately document what is being covered and what happened in the weekly meetings?

5. Do you understand the quality and control criteria that must be achieved for successful Web Technologies and APIs project completion?

6. Measurable - Are the targets measurable?

7. What are the constraints?

8. Do you understand the communication expectations for this Web Technologies and APIs project?

9. Realistic - Are the desired results expressed in a way that the team will be motivated and believe that the

required level of involvement will be obtained?

10. Who are the Web Technologies and APIs project stakeholders?

11. Professionals want to know what is expected from them what are the deliverables?

12. Are identified risks being monitored properly, are new risks arising during the Web Technologies and APIs project or are foreseen risks occurring?

13. Were sponsors and decision makers available when needed outside regularly scheduled meetings?

14. Are there resources to maintain and support the outcome of the Web Technologies and APIs project?

15. How well defined and documented were the Web Technologies and APIs project management processes you chose to use?

16. How should their needs be met?

17. How to control and approve each phase?

18. Will the Web Technologies and APIs project meet the client requirements, and will it achieve the business success criteria that justified doing the Web Technologies and APIs project in the first place?

19. How can I make my needs known?

20. Who does what?

1.1 Project Charter: Web Technologies and APIs

21. Who will take notes, document decisions?

22. Who are the stakeholders?

23. Market – Identify products market, including whether it is outside of the objective: What is the purpose of the program or Web Technologies and APIs project?

24. When is a charter needed?

25. What date will the task finish?

26. Fit with other Products Compliments – Cannibalizes?

27. Will this replace an existing product?

28. When will this occur?

29. Why have you chosen the aim you have set forth?

30. How are Web Technologies and APIs projects different from Operations?

31. For whom?

32. Where does all this information come from?

33. Why Executive Support?

34. Avoid costs, improve service, and/ or comply with a mandate?

35. Why use a Web Technologies and APIs project charter?

36. What does it need to do?

37. Who Manages Integration?

38. Whose input and support will this Web Technologies and APIs project require?

39. When?

40. Name and describe the elements that deal with providing the detail?

1.2 Stakeholder Register: Web Technologies and APIs

41. Who is Managing Stakeholder Engagement?

42. Who wants to talk about Security?

43. How Big is the Gap?

44. What is the power of the stakeholder?

45. What are the major Web Technologies and APIs project milestones requiring communications or providing communications opportunities?

46. What & Why?

47. How will Reports Be Created?

48. Is Your Organization Ready for Change?

49. How much influence do they have on the Web Technologies and APIs project?

50. How should employers make their voices heard?

51. What opportunities exist to provide communications?

1.3 Stakeholder Analysis Matrix: Web Technologies and APIs

52. Inoculations or payment to receive them?

53. What tools would help us communicate?

54. Opponents; Who are the opponents?

55. Continuity, supply chain robustness?

56. Who holds positions of responsibility in interested organizations?

57. Why involve the stakeholder?

58. What is Social & Public Accountability ?

59. Who will obstruct/hinder the Web Technologies and APIs project if they are not involved?

60. What is the organizations competitors doing?

61. Environmental effects?

62. What do people from other organizations see as our strengths?

63. Loss of key staff?

64. How do you manage Web Technologies and APIs project Risk?

65. Why do you need to manage Web Technologies and APIs project Risk?

66. Benefit to whom?

67. Own known vulnerabilities?

68. Alliances: With which other actors is the actor allied, how are they interconnected?

69. Accreditations, etc?

70. Reputation, presence and reach?

71. Who influences whom?

2.0 Planning Process Group: Web Technologies and APIs

72. What is a Software Development Life Cycle (SDLC)?

73. What is involved in Web Technologies and APIs project scope management, and why is good Web Technologies and APIs project scope management so important on information technology Web Technologies and APIs projects?

74. Just how important is your work to the overall success of the Web Technologies and APIs project?

75. What Business Situation Is Being Addressed?

76. To what extent have public/private national resources and/or counterparts been mobilized to contribute to the programmes objective and produce results and impacts?

77. Is the pace of implementing the products of the programme ensuring the completeness of the results of the Web Technologies and APIs project?

78. What are the different approaches to building the WBS?

79. On which process should team members spend the most time?

80. Will you be replaced?

81. When developing the estimates for Web Technologies and APIs project phases, you choose to add the individual estimates for the activities that comprise each phase. What type of estimation method are you using?

82. Is the identification of the problems, inequalities and gaps, with their respective causes, clear in the Web Technologies and APIs project?

83. Professionals want to know what is expected from them; what are the deliverables?

84. How many days can task X be late in starting without affecting the Web Technologies and APIs project completion date?

85. To what extent have the target population and participants made the activities their own, taking an active role in it?

86. If you are late, will anybody notice?

87. Contingency planning. If a risk event occurs, what will you do?

88. If task X starts two days late, what is the effect on the Web Technologies and APIs project end date?

89. When will the Web Technologies and APIs project be done?

90. What good practices or successful experiences or transferable examples have been identified?

91. Is the Web Technologies and APIs project

supported by national and/or local organizations?

2.1 Project Management Plan: Web Technologies and APIs

92. Will you add a schedule and diagram?

93. What data/reports/tools/etc. do program managers need?

94. Does the implementation plan have an appropriate division of responsibilities?

95. What data/reports/tools/etc. do your PMs need?

96. What worked well?

97. How well are you able to manage your risk?

98. What are the deliverables?

99. Was the peer (technical) review of the cost estimates duly coordinated with the cost estimate center of expertise and addressed in the review documentation and certification?

100. What are the assigned resources?

101. Are calculations and results of analyses essentially correct?

102. What is risk management?

103. Is the appropriate plan selected based on the organizations objectives and evaluation criteria

expressed in Principles and Guidelines policies?

104. Are the existing and future without-plan conditions reasonable and appropriate?

105. Why Do you Manage Integration?

106. Is the budget realistic?

107. What did not work so well?

108. What Went Right?

109. Is mitigation authorized or recommended?

110. Why Change?

2.2 Scope Management Plan: Web Technologies and APIs

111. For which criterion is it tolerable not to meet the original parameters?

112. Have all team members been part of identifying risks?

113. Organizational unit (e.g., department, team, or person) who will accept responsibility for satisfactory completion of the item?

114. Is there a formal set of procedures supporting Issues Management?

115. Do Web Technologies and APIs project managers participating in the Web Technologies and APIs project know the Web Technologies and APIs projects true status first hand?

116. Who is doing what for whom?

117. Do all stakeholders know how to access this repository and where to find the Web Technologies and APIs project documentation?

118. Have all unresolved risks been documented?

119. Product – what are you trying to accomplish and how will you know when you are finished?

120. Have all documents been archived in a Web

Technologies and APIs project repository for each release?

121. Has stakeholder analysis been conducted, assessing their influence on the Web Technologies and APIs project and their authority levels?

122. How do you handle uncertainty or conflict?

123. Are the Web Technologies and APIs project plans updated on a frequent basis?

124. Have the personnel with the necessary skills and competence been identified and has agreement for their participation in the Web Technologies and APIs project been reached with the appropriate management?

125. Are multiple estimation methods being employed?

126. Are you spending the right amount of money for specific tasks?

127. Has adequate time for orientation & training of Web Technologies and APIs project staff been provided for in relation to technical nature of the application and the experience levels of Web Technologies and APIs project personnel?

128. Are assumptions being identified, recorded, analyzed, qualified and closed?

129. Has the budget been baselined?

2.3 Requirements Management Plan: Web Technologies and APIs

130. Do you expect stakeholders to be cooperative?

131. How knowledgeable is the primary Stakeholder(s) in the proposed application area?

132. Will the contractors involved take full responsibility?

133. Does the Web Technologies and APIs project have a Change Control process?

134. Are actual resource expenditures versus planned still acceptable?

135. How do you know that you have done this right?

136. Will the Web Technologies and APIs project requirements become approved in writing?

137. Subject to Change Control?

138. Did you get proper approvals?

139. Do you really need to write this document at all?

140. Who will finally present the work or product(s) for acceptance?

141. What is a problem?

142. Who will perform the analysis?

143. Are all the stakeholders ready for the transition into the user community?

144. Which hardware or software, related to, or as outcome of the Web Technologies and APIs project is new to the organization?

145. Is infrastructure setup part of your Web Technologies and APIs project?

146. Is the system software (non-operating system) new to the IT Web Technologies and APIs project team?

147. How will you develop the schedule of requirements activities?

148. What performance metrics will be used?

2.4 Requirements Documentation: Web Technologies and APIs

149. What is a show stopper in the requirements?

150. What is the risk associated with the technology?

151. Where are business rules being captured?

152. Verifiability. Can the requirements be checked?

153. What are the attributes of a customer?

154. Is the origin of the requirement clearly stated?

155. Who is interacting with the system?

156. What are the potential disadvantages/ advantages?

157. How can you document system requirements?

158. What kind of entity is a problem ?

159. What is your Elevator Speech?

160. What are current process problems?

161. What is Effective documentation?

162. How will Requirements be documented and who signs off on them?

163. How will the proposed Web Technologies and APIs project help?

164. How will they be documented / shared?

165. If applicable; are there issues linked with the fact that this is an offshore Web Technologies and APIs project?

166. What images does it conjure?

167. What variations exist for a process?

2.5 Requirements Traceability Matrix: Web Technologies and APIs

168. What is the WBS?

169. How will it affect the stakeholders personally in their career?

170. How small is small enough?

171. What are the chronologies, contingencies, consequences, criteria?

172. Will you use a Requirements Traceability Matrix?

173. Why use a WBS?

174. Describe the process for approving requirements so they can be added to the traceability matrix and Web Technologies and APIs project work can be performed. Will the Web Technologies and APIs project requirements become approved in writing?

175. How Do you Manage Scope?

176. Is there a requirements traceability process in place?

177. Do we have a clear understanding of all subcontracts in place?

178. Why Do you Manage Scope?

179. What percentage of Web Technologies and APIs projects are producing traceability matrices between requirements and other work products?

2.6 Project Scope Statement: Web Technologies and APIs

180. Is an Issue Management Process documented and filed?

181. Was planning completed before the Web Technologies and APIs project was initiated?

182. Name and describe the 2 elements that deal with providing the detail?

183. Relevant - ask yourself can you get there; why are we doing this Web Technologies and APIs project?

184. What should you drop in order to add something new?

185. Is there an information system for the Web Technologies and APIs project?

186. Has a method and process for requirement tracking been developed?

187. What Went Wrong?

188. If the scope changes, what will the impact be to your Web Technologies and APIs project in terms of duration, cost, quality, or any other important areas of the Web Technologies and APIs project?

189. What are the possible consequences should a risk come to occur?

190. Are there issues that could affect the existing requirements for the result, service, or product if the scope changes?

191. Is the Web Technologies and APIs project organization documented and on file?

192. Name the 2 elements of scope management that deal with concept development ?

193. Is the plan for Web Technologies and APIs project resources adequate?

194. Are there backup strategies for key members of the Web Technologies and APIs project?

195. Has the Web Technologies and APIs project Scope Statement been reviewed as part of the baseline process?

196. Which Risks Does the Web Technologies and APIs project Focus On?

197. Has everyone approved the Web Technologies and APIs projects scope statement?

198. What is a process you might recommend to verify the accuracy of the research deliverable?

2.7 Assumption and Constraint Log: Web Technologies and APIs

199. Contradictory information between document sections?

200. Is the Steering Committee active in Web Technologies and APIs project oversight?

201. Are processes for release management of new development from coding and unit testing, to integration testing, to training, and production defined and followed?

202. If appropriate, is the deliverable content consistent with current Web Technologies and APIs project documents and in compliance with the Document Management Plan?

203. Are you meeting our customers expectations consistently?

204. Would known impacts serve as impediments?

205. Are there processes defining how software will be developed including development methods, overall timeline for development, software product standards, and traceability?

206. Are there processes in place to ensure that all the terms and code concepts have been documented consistently?

207. Are there nonconformance issues?

208. Have all involved stakeholders and work groups committed to the Web Technologies and APIs project?

209. Is there documentation of system capability requirements, data requirements, environment requirements, security requirements, and computer and hardware requirements?

210. Are there processes in place to ensure internal consistency between the source code components?

211. What Strengths do you have?

212. Are there procedures in place to effectively manage interdependencies with other Web Technologies and APIs projects / systems?

213. Does the traceability documentation describe the tool and/or mechanism to be used to capture traceability throughout the life cycle?

214. How relevant is this attribute to this Web Technologies and APIs project or audit?

215. Does the document/deliverable meet general requirements (for example, statement of work) for all deliverables?

216. What do you audit?

217. Do the requirements meet the standards of correctness, completeness, consistency, accuracy, and readability?

2.8 Work Breakdown Structure: Web Technologies and APIs

218. When would you develop a Work Breakdown Structure?

219. How much detail?

220. How Far Down?

221. What is the probability of completing the Web Technologies and APIs project in less that xx days?

222. How will you and your Web Technologies and APIs project team define the Web Technologies and APIs projects scope and work breakdown structure?

223. Can you make it?

224. Why is it useful?

225. Do you need another level?

226. How many levels?

227. Is it still viable?

228. What has to be done?

229. Who has to do it?

230. How big is a work-package?

231. What is the probability that the Web Technologies and APIs project duration will exceed xx weeks?

232. Why would you develop a Work Breakdown Structure?

233. Where does it take place?

234. When do you stop?

235. Is the Work breakdown Structure (WBS) defined and is the scope of the Web Technologies and APIs project clear with assigned deliverable owners?

236. Is it a change in scope?

237. When does it have to be done?

2.9 WBS Dictionary: Web Technologies and APIs

238. Does the contractors system provide for accurate cost accumulation and assignment to control accounts in a manner consistent with the budgets using recognized acceptable costing techniques?

239. Does the scheduling system identify in a timely manner the status of work?

240. Are overhead costs budgets established on a basis consistent with anticipated direct business base?

241. Are estimates developed by Web Technologies and APIs project personnel coordinated with those responsible for overall management to determine whether required resources will be available according to revised planning?

242. Are material costs reported within the same period as that in which BCWP is earned for that material?

243. Does the contractors system include procedures for measuring performance of the lowest level organization responsible for the control account?

244. Is future work which cannot be planned in detail subdivided to the extent practicable for budgeting and scheduling purposes?

245. Appropriate work authorization documents which subdivide the contractual effort and responsibilities, within functional organizations?

246. The Web Technologies and APIs projected business base for each period?

247. Budgets assigned to control accounts?

248. Budgets assigned to major functional organizations?

249. Are all authorized tasks assigned to identified organizational elements?

250. Are direct or indirect cost adjustments being accomplished according to accounting procedures acceptable to us?

251. Are time-phased budgets established for planning and control of level of effort activity by category of resource; for example, type of manpower and/or material?

252. Are records maintained to show how undistributed budgets are controlled?

253. Are the contractors estimates of costs at completion reconcilable with cost data reported to us?

254. Are control accounts opened and closed based on the start and completion of work contained therein?

2.10 Schedule Management Plan: Web Technologies and APIs

255. Have external dependencies been captured in the schedule?

256. Does the IMS include all contract and/or designated management control milestones?

257. Were Web Technologies and APIs project team members involved in detailed estimating and scheduling?

258. Has a Quality Assurance Plan been developed for the Web Technologies and APIs project?

259. Are any non-compliance issues that exist due to the organizations practices communicated to the organization?

260. Has the Web Technologies and APIs project manager been identified?

261. Are procurement deliverables arriving on time and to specification?

262. Is there a Steering Committee in place?

263. Have key stakeholders been identified?

264. Are meeting minutes captured and sent out after the meeting?

265. Are trade-offs between accepting the risk and mitigating the risk identified?

266. Are the primary and secondary schedule tools defined?

267. Is there a set of procedures defining the scope, procedures, and deliverables defining quality control?

268. What happens if a warning is triggered?

269. What tools and techniques will be used to estimate activity durations?

270. Are all attributes of the activities defined, including risk and uncertainty?

271. Are individual tasks of reasonable time effort (8–40 hours)?

272. Pareto diagrams, statistical sampling, flow charting or trend analysis used quality monitoring?

273. Were Web Technologies and APIs project team members involved in the development of activity & task decomposition?

274. Can be realistically shortened (the duration of subsequent tasks)?

2.11 Activity List: Web Technologies and APIs

275. Is there anything planned that doesn t need to be here?

276. What went well?

277. Who will perform the work?

278. How detailed should a Web Technologies and APIs project get?

279. What is the probability the Web Technologies and APIs project can be completed in xx weeks?

280. When will the work be performed?

281. How will it be performed?

282. What are you counting on?

283. Should you include sub-activities?

284. Is infrastructure setup part of your Web Technologies and APIs project?

285. Are the required resources available or need to be acquired?

286. Where will it be performed?

287. What did not go as well?

288. For other activities, how much delay can be tolerated?

289. What will be performed?

290. What is the least expensive way to complete the Web Technologies and APIs project within 40 weeks?

291. The WBS is developed as part of a Joint Planning session. But how do you know that youve done this right?

292. What is the organization s history in doing similar activities?

2.12 Activity Attributes: Web Technologies and APIs

293. Do you feel very comfortable with your prediction?

294. Where else does it apply?

295. Can you re-assign any activities to another resource to resolve an over-allocation?

296. Activity: Fair or Not Fair?

297. Can more resources be added?

298. Whats Missing?

299. How difficult will it be to do specific activities on this Web Technologies and APIs project?

300. Is there a trend during the year?

301. Were there other ways you could have organized the data to achieve similar results?

302. How difficult will it be to complete specific activities on this Web Technologies and APIs project?

303. Are the required resources available?

304. Activity: Whats In the Bag?

305. Which method produces the more accurate cost

assignment?

306. How many days do you need to complete the work scope with a limit of X number of resources?

307. How else could the items be grouped?

308. Whats the general pattern here?

2.13 Milestone List: Web Technologies and APIs

309. Reliability of data, plan predictability?

310. When will the Web Technologies and APIs project be complete?

311. Describe the industry you are in and the market growth opportunities. What is the market for your technology, product or service?

312. How will the milestone be verified?

313. Which path is the critical path?

314. Level of the Innovation?

315. Obstacles faced?

316. What has been done so far?

317. Can you derive how soon can the whole Web Technologies and APIs project finish?

318. What specific improvements did you make to the Web Technologies and APIs project proposal since the previous time?

319. Calculate how long can activity be delayed?

320. Political effects?

321. How Do you Manage Time?

322. How difficult will it be to do specific activities on this Web Technologies and APIs project?

323. Sustaining internal capabilities?

324. Do you foresee any technical risks or developmental challenges?

325. Describe the companys strengths and core competencies. What factors will make the company succeed?

2.14 Network Diagram: Web Technologies and APIs

326. Are you on time?

327. Can you calculate the confidence level?

328. What to do and When?

329. Exercise: What is the probability that the Web Technologies and APIs project duration will exceed xx weeks?

330. Are the Gantt Chart and/or Network Diagram updated periodically and used to assess the overall Web Technologies and APIs project timetable?

331. What activities must follow this activity?

332. What are the tools?

333. What is the lowest cost to complete this Web Technologies and APIs project in xx weeks?

334. Will crashing x weeks return more in benefits than it costs?

335. What job or jobs precede it?

336. Where Do Schedules Come From?

337. How difficult will it be to do specific activities on this Web Technologies and APIs project?

338. Planning: who, how long, what to do?

339. Where do you schedule uncertainty time?

340. What is the probability of completing the Web Technologies and APIs project in less that xx days?

341. Review the logical flow of the network diagram. Take a look at which activities you have first and then sequence the activities. Do they make sense?

342. What can be done concurrently?

343. What activity must be completed immediately before this activity can start?

2.15 Activity Resource Requirements: Web Technologies and APIs

344. Are there unresolved issues that need to be addressed?

345. How do you handle petty cash?

346. How many signatures do you require on a check and does this match what is in your policy and procedures?

347. What are constraints that you might find during the Human Resource Planning process?

348. Which logical relationship does the PDM use most often?

349. Do you use tools like decomposition and rolling-wave planning to produce the activity list and other outputs?

350. Organizational Applicability?

351. Why do you do that?

352. Time for overtime?

353. Anything else?

354. When does Monitoring Begin?

355. Other support in specific areas?

356. What is the Work Plan Standard?

2.16 Resource Breakdown Structure: Web Technologies and APIs

357. What s the difference between % Complete and % work?

358. What are the requirements for resource data?

359. What is the organizations history in doing similar activities?

360. What can you do to improve productivity?

361. Who is allowed to perform which functions?

362. Who will use the system?

363. What Defines a Successful Web Technologies and APIs project?

364. How difficult will it be to do specific activities on this Web Technologies and APIs project?

365. What is the primary purpose of the human resource plan?

366. The list could probably go on, but, the thing that you would most like to know is, How long & How much?

367. Is Predictive Resource Analysis being done?

368. Which resources should be in the resource pool?

369. Who delivers the information?

370. How should the information be delivered?

371. Why Do you Do It?

372. What Is Web Technologies and APIs project Communication Management?

2.17 Activity Duration Estimates: Web Technologies and APIs

373. What are the three main outputs of quality control?

374. What tasks must precede this task?

375. Do you think many information technology professionals have experience writing RFPs and evaluating proposals for information technology Web Technologies and APIs projects?

376. Which includes asking team members about the time estimates for their activities and reaching agreement on the calendar date for each activity?

377. Which skills do you think are most important for an information technology Web Technologies and APIs project manager?

378. How does the job market and current state of the economy affect human resource management?

379. Are the causes of all variances identified?

380. Do scope statements include the Web Technologies and APIs project objectives and expected deliverables?

381. What are some crucial elements of a good Web Technologies and APIs project plan?

382. Have most organizations benefited from outsourcing?

383. Who will provide training for the new application?

384. What type of contract was used and why?

385. How many different communications channels does a Web Technologies and APIs project team with six people have?

386. Find an example of a contract for information technology services. Analyze the key features of the contract. What type of contract was used and why?

387. What functions does this software provide that cannot be done easily using other tools such as a spreadsheet or database?

388. What is WRONG with this scenario?

389. Do they make sense?

390. What questions do you have about the sample documents provided?

391. How have experts such as Deming, Juran, Crosby, and Taguchi affected the quality movement and todays use of Six Sigma?

2.18 Duration Estimating Worksheet: Web Technologies and APIs

392. Does the Web Technologies and APIs project provide innovative ways for Veterans to overcome obstacles or deliver better outcomes?

393. Value Pocket Identification & Quantification What Are Value Pockets?

394. How should ongoing costs be monitored to try to keep the Web Technologies and APIs project within budget?

395. Is this operation cost effective?

396. Done before proceeding with this activity or what can be done concurrently?

397. What is the total time required to complete the Web Technologies and APIs project if no delays occur?

398. When does the organization expect to be able to complete it?

399. What s an Average Web Technologies and APIs project?

400. Do any colleagues have experience with the company and/or RFPs?

401. Small or Large Web Technologies and APIs project?

402. Is a Construction detail attached (to aid in explanation)?

403. What s Next?

404. Why Estimate Costs?

405. What is the least expensive way to complete the Web Technologies and APIs project within 40 weeks?

406. What work will be included in the Web Technologies and APIs project?

407. Will the Web Technologies and APIs project collaborate with the local community and leverage resources?

408. When, then?

409. What questions do you have?

410. Is the Web Technologies and APIs project responsive to community need?

2.19 Project Schedule: Web Technologies and APIs

411. Meet requirements?

412. How can you fix it?

413. How detailed should a Web Technologies and APIs project get?

414. Why do you need to manage Web Technologies and APIs project Risk?

415. How Do you Use Schedules?

416. It allows the Web Technologies and APIs project to be delivered on schedule. How Do you Use Schedules?

417. Why is this particularly bad?

418. How can you shorten the schedule?

419. Did the final product meet or exceed user expectations?

420. If you can t fix it, how do you do it differently?

421. What is Web Technologies and APIs project Management?

422. How long does a 12 month Web Technologies and APIs project take?

423. To what degree is do you feel the entire team was committed to the Web Technologies and APIs project schedule?

424. How can you minimize or control changes to Web Technologies and APIs project schedules?

425. Web Technologies and APIs project work estimates Who is managing the work estimate quality of work tasks in the Web Technologies and APIs project schedule?

2.20 Cost Management Plan: Web Technologies and APIs

426. Has Web Technologies and APIs project success criteria been defined?

427. Are internal Web Technologies and APIs project status meetings held at reasonable intervals?

428. Is the structure for tracking the Web Technologies and APIs project schedule well defined and assigned to a specific individual?

429. Are estimating assumptions and constraints captured?

430. Are milestone deliverables effectively tracked and compared to Web Technologies and APIs project plan?

431. Is there a requirements change management processes in place?

432. Are target dates established for each milestone deliverable?

433. What Is Web Technologies and APIs project Management?

434. Are cause and effect determined for risks when others occur?

435. Are enough systems & user personnel assigned

to the Web Technologies and APIs project?

436. Is there an onboarding process in place?

437. Were stakeholders aware and supportive of the principles and practices of modern software estimation?

438. Change types and category – What are the types of changes and what are the techniques to report and control changes?

439. Escalation Criteria Met?

440. Has a Quality Assurance Plan been developed for the Web Technologies and APIs project?

441. Contingency rundown curve be used on the Web Technologies and APIs project?

442. Are written status reports provided on a designated frequent basis?

443. How relevant is this attribute to this Web Technologies and APIs project or audit?

444. For example, will the forecasts be based on trend analysis and earned value statistics?

445. Has a capability assessment been conducted?

2.21 Activity Cost Estimates: Web Technologies and APIs

446. What is the Web Technologies and APIs projects sustainability strategy that will ensure Web Technologies and APIs project results will endure or be sustained?

447. Were the costs or charges reasonable?

448. Is there anything unique in this Web Technologies and APIs project s scope statement that will affect resources?

449. How do I fund change orders?

450. Who determines when the contractor is paid?

451. Are cost subtotals needed?

452. What is a Web Technologies and APIs project Management Plan?

453. What are you looking for?

454. Review – what are some common errors in activities to avoid?

455. Why Do you Manage Cost?

456. What is the estimators estimating history?

457. What is the organization s history in doing similar

tasks?

458. Were the tasks or work products prepared by the consultant useful?

459. What makes a good activity description?

460. Can you change our activities?

461. Does the estimator estimate by task or by person?

462. If you are asked to lower your estimate because the price is too high, what are your options?

463. Was the consultant knowledgeable about the program?

464. Does the activity use a common approach or business function to deliver its results?

2.22 Cost Estimating Worksheet: Web Technologies and APIs

465. What happens to any remaining funds not used?

466. Will the Web Technologies and APIs project collaborate with the local community and leverage resources?

467. What additional Web Technologies and APIs project(s) could be initiated as a result of this Web Technologies and APIs project?

468. What info is needed?

469. What will others want?

470. Ask: are others positioned to know, are others credible, and will others cooperate?

471. How will the results be shared and to whom?

472. Identify the timeframe necessary to monitor progress and collect data to determine how the selected measure has changed?

473. Is the Web Technologies and APIs project responsive to community need?

474. What is the purpose of estimating?

475. Does the Web Technologies and APIs project provide innovative ways for stakeholders to overcome

obstacles or deliver better outcomes?

476. What Can Be Included?

477. Is it feasible to establish a control group arrangement?

478. What costs are to be estimated?

479. What is the estimated labor cost today based upon this information?

480. Can a trend be established from historical performance data on the selected measure and are the criteria for using trend analysis or forecasting methods met?

481. Who is best positioned to know and assist in identifying such factors?

2.23 Cost Baseline: Web Technologies and APIs

482. Should a more thorough impact analysis be conducted?

483. What can go wrong?

484. Has the Web Technologies and APIs projected annual cost to operate and maintain the product(s) or service(s) been approved and funded?

485. Have the resources used by the Web Technologies and APIs project been reassigned to other units or Web Technologies and APIs projects?

486. On time?

487. What s the reality?

488. What is the most important thing to do next to make your Web Technologies and APIs project successful?

489. When should cost estimates be developed?

490. Review your risk triggers -have your risks changed?

491. Vac -variance at completion, how much over/ under budget do you expect to be?

492. How long are you willing to wait before you find

out were late?

493. How difficult will it be to do specific tasks on the Web Technologies and APIs project?

494. Has the actual cost of the Web Technologies and APIs project (or Web Technologies and APIs project phase) been tallied and compared to the approved budget?

495. At which frequency ?

496. Does the suggested change request represent a desired enhancement to the products functionality?

497. How accurate do cost estimates need to be?

498. What would some of the life cycle costs be?

499. Does it impact schedule, cost, quality?

2.24 Quality Management Plan: Web Technologies and APIs

500. How are training records kept?

501. How do you ensure that your sampling methods and procedures meet your data needs?

502. Do trained quality assurance auditors conduct the audits as defined in the Quality Management Plan and scheduled by the Web Technologies and APIs project manager?

503. How will you know that a change is actually an improvement?

504. How relevant is this attribute to this Web Technologies and APIs project or audit?

505. What procedures are used to determine if you use, and the number of split, replicate or duplicate samples taken at a site?

506. What key performance indicators does your organization use to measure, manage, and improve key processes?

507. What other teams / processes would be impacted by changes to the current process, and how?

508. Is there a procedure for this process?

509. How long do you retain data?

510. How do your action plans support the strategic objectives?

511. Have all involved stakeholders and work groups committed to the Web Technologies and APIs project?

512. How does your organization decide what to measure?

513. How effectively was the Quality Management Plan applied during Web Technologies and APIs project Execution?

514. Does a documented Web Technologies and APIs project organizational policy & plan (i.e. governance model) exist?

515. What type of in-house testing do you conduct?

516. Were there any deficiencies / issues in prior years self-assessment?

517. How is staff trained in procedures?

518. Who Else Should Be Involved ?

519. Do the data quality objectives communicate the intended program need?

2.25 Quality Metrics: Web Technologies and APIs

520. Which are the right metrics to use?

521. Can you correlate your quality metrics to profitability?

522. Are interface issues coordinated?

523. When is the security analysis testing complete?

524. How exactly do you define when differences exist?

525. Is Quality Culture a competitive advantage?

526. What about still open problems?

527. How are requirements conflicts resolved?

528. Which data do others need in one place to target areas of improvement?

529. Are there any open risk issues?

530. Does risk analysis documentation meet standards?

531. Are there already quality metrics available that detect nonlinear embeddings and trends similar to the users perception?

532. Which report did you use to create the data you are submitting?

533. What group is empowered to define quality requirements?

534. How effective are your security tests?

535. Who is willing to lead?

536. Is there a set of procedures to capture, analyze and act on quality metrics?

537. Did evaluation start on time?

538. How do you know if everyone is trying to improve the right things?

2.26 Process Improvement Plan: Web Technologies and APIs

539. Why do you want to achieve the goal?

540. Does explicit definition of the measures exist?

541. Has the time line required to move measurement results from the points of collection to databases or users been established?

542. To elicit goal statements, do you ask a question such as, What do you want to achieve?

543. Has a process guide to collect the data been developed?

544. Are there forms and procedures to collect and record the data?

545. Where do you want to be?

546. What makes people good SPI coaches?

547. What personnel are the coaches for your initiative?

548. Why Quality Management?

549. What personnel are the change agents for your initiative?

550. Does our process ensure quality?

551. How Do you Manage Quality?

552. What is quality and how will you ensure it?

553. Have the frequency of collection and the points in the process where measurements will be made been determined?

554. Who should prepare the process improvement action plan?

555. What Actions Are Needed to Address the Problems and Achieve the Goals?

556. Are you following the quality standards?

557. Everyone agrees on what process improvement is, right?

558. Are you Making Progress on the Goals?

2.27 Responsibility Assignment Matrix: Web Technologies and APIs

559. Are significant decision points, constraints, and interfaces identified as key milestones?

560. Is the anticipated (firm and potential) business base Web Technologies and APIs projected in a rational, consistent manner?

561. Wbs elements contractually specified for reporting of status (lowest level only)?

562. Are detailed work packages planned as far in advance as practicable?

563. What is the business need?

564. Budgeted cost for work performed?

565. Are indirect costs charged to the appropriate indirect pools and incurring organization?

566. What simple tool can you use to help identify and prioritize Web Technologies and APIs project risks thats very low tech and high touch?

567. The staff characteristics – is the group or the person capable to work together as a team?

568. Detailed schedules which support control account and work package start and completion dates/events?

569. Does each activity-deliverable have exactly one Accountable responsibility, so that accountability is clear and decisions can be made quickly?

570. Does the contractors system provide unit or lot costs when applicable?

2.28 Roles and Responsibilities: Web Technologies and APIs

571. Be specific; avoid generalities. Thank you and great work alone are insufficient. What exactly do you appreciate and why?

572. What should you highlight for improvement?

573. What specific behaviors did you observe?

574. Do you take the time to clearly define roles and responsibilities on Web Technologies and APIs project tasks?

575. What areas would you highlight for changes or improvements?

576. How well did the Web Technologies and APIs project Team understand the expectations of specific roles and responsibilities?

577. Do the values and practices inherent in the culture of the organization foster or hinder the process?

578. Attainable / Achievable: The goal is attainable; can you actually accomplish the goal?

579. Are Web Technologies and APIs project team roles and responsibilities identified and documented?

580. Where are you most strong as a supervisor?

581. Who is responsible for implementation activities and where will the functions, roles and responsibilities be defined?

582. Implementation of actions: Who are the responsible units?

583. Is the data complete?

584. To decide whether to use a quality measurement, ask how will I know when it is achieved?

585. Are our budgets supportive of a culture of quality data?

586. Authority: What areas/Web Technologies and APIs projects in your work do you have the authority to decide upon and act on those decisions?

587. Who is involved?

588. Who is responsible for each task?

589. Have you ever been a part of this team?

590. Once the responsibilities are defined for the Web Technologies and APIs project, have the deliverables, roles and responsibilities been clearly communicated to every participant?

2.29 Human Resource Management Plan: Web Technologies and APIs

591. Is the firm certified as a supplier, wholesaler, regular dealer, or manufacturer of such products/supplies?

592. Were stakeholders aware and supportive of the principles and practices of modern cost estimation?

593. Has a Quality Assurance Plan been developed for the Web Technologies and APIs project?

594. Cost / Benefit Analysis?

595. Is it possible to track all classes of Web Technologies and APIs project work (e.g. scheduled, un-scheduled, defect repair, etc.)?

596. Responsiveness to change and the resulting demands for different skills and abilities?

597. Is Web Technologies and APIs project work proceeding in accordance with the original Web Technologies and APIs project schedule?

598. Are milestone deliverables effectively tracked and compared to Web Technologies and APIs project plan?

599. Who Needs Training?

600. Have all involved Web Technologies and APIs

project stakeholders and work groups committed to the Web Technologies and APIs project?

601. Has a structured approach been used to break work effort into manageable components (WBS)?

602. Is there a formal process for updating the Web Technologies and APIs project baseline?

603. How to convince employees that this is a necessary process?

604. Are enough systems & user personnel assigned to the Web Technologies and APIs project?

605. Does the Business Case include how the Web Technologies and APIs project aligns with the organizations strategic goals & objectives?

606. Have reserves been created to address risks?

607. Is the current culture aligned with the vision, mission, and values of the department?

608. Are mitigation strategies identified?

609. Who are the people that make up the company and whom create the success that the company enjoys as a whole?

2.30 Communications Management Plan: Web Technologies and APIs

610. Conflict Resolution -which method when?

611. Which stakeholders are thought leaders, influences, or early adopters?

612. How much time does it take to do it?

613. Are stakeholders internal or external?

614. How will the person responsible for executing the communication item be notified?

615. Are you constantly rushing from meeting to meeting?

616. Who did you turn to if you had questions?

617. What to learn?

618. Why Do you Manage Communications?

619. Who to share with?

620. Will messages be directly related to the release strategy or phases of the Web Technologies and APIs project?

621. Can you think of other people who might have concerns or interests?

622. What are the interrelationships?

623. What to know?

624. Are there potential barriers between the team and the stakeholder?

625. Who is responsible?

626. What is the political influence?

627. Which stakeholders can influence others?

628. Who needs to know and how much?

629. How often do you engage with stakeholders?

2.31 Risk Management Plan: Web Technologies and APIs

630. What should be done with non-critical risks?

631. Have staff received necessary training?

632. Are flexibility and reuse paramount?

633. What risks are necessary to achieve success?

634. What is the likelihood that the organization would accept responsibility for the risk?

635. What is the likelihood?

636. How is Implementation of Risk Actions Performed?

637. How would you suggest monitoring for risk transition indicators?

638. Should the risk be taken at all?

639. What are the chances the risk event will occur?

640. Do the people have the right combinations of skills?

641. A determination to transfer a risk may be made during which step of risk management?

642. How Is The Audit Profession Changing?

643. Is the customer willing to participate in reviews?

644. For software; Are compilers and code generators available and suitable for the product to be built?

645. Is there additional information that would make you more confident about your analysis?

646. Why Is Product Liability a Serious Issue?

647. Does the Web Technologies and APIs project team have experience with the technology to be implemented?

648. Does the customer understand the software process?

649. Technology risk: Is the Web Technologies and APIs project technically feasible?

2.32 Risk Register: Web Technologies and APIs

650. Are there any gaps in the evidence?

651. Financial risk -can the organization afford to undertake the Web Technologies and APIs project?

652. What is the reason for current performance gaps and do the risks and opportunities identified previously explain this?

653. What evidence do you have to justify the likelihood score of the risk (audit, incident report, claim, complaints, inspection, internal review)?

654. Who is accountable?

655. How often will the Risk Management Plan and Risk Register be formally reviewed, and by whom?

656. Risk Categories: What are the main categories of risks that should be addressed on this Web Technologies and APIs project?

657. Can the likelihood and impact of failing to achieve such recommendations and action plans be assessed?

658. What may happen or not go according to plan?

659. Manageability – Have mitigations to the risk been identified?

660. Severity Prediction?

661. What is the probability and impact of the risk occurring?

662. What are you going to do to limit the Web Technologies and APIs projects risk exposure due to the identified risks?

663. What further options might be available for responding to the risk?

664. Technology risk -is the Web Technologies and APIs project technically feasible?

665. Having taken action, how did the responses effect change, and where is the Web Technologies and APIs project now?

666. What could prevent us delivering on the strategic program objectives and what is being done to mitigate such issues?

667. Assume the risk event or situation happens, what would the impact be?

668. What can be done about it?

669. What action, if any, has been taken to respond to the risk?

2.33 Probability and Impact Assessment: Web Technologies and APIs

670. How will the consumption pattern change?

671. What are the uncertainties associated with the technology selected for the Web Technologies and APIs project?

672. What will be cost of redeployment of personnel?

673. What can you do to minimize the impact if it does?

674. What would be the effect of slippage?

675. How much risk do others need to take?

676. My Web Technologies and APIs project leader has suddenly left the company, what do I do?

677. Is the customer technically sophisticated in the product area?

678. What will be the impact or consequence if the risk occurs?

679. Is the customer willing to establish rapid communication links with the developer?

680. Which role do you have in the Web Technologies and APIs project?

681. Can this technology be absorbed with current level of expertise available in the organization?

682. What are its business ethics?

683. What are the tools and techniques used in managing the challenges faced?

684. Assuming that you have identified a number of risks in the Web Technologies and APIs project, how would you prioritize them?

685. When and how will the recent breakthroughs in basic research lead to commercial products?

686. Have you ascribed a level of confidence to every critical technical objective?

2.34 Probability and Impact Matrix: Web Technologies and APIs

687. What will be the likely political situation during the life of the Web Technologies and APIs project?

688. What should be the gestation period for the Web Technologies and APIs project with this technology?

689. What action would you take to the identified risks in the Web Technologies and APIs project?

690. What will be the likely incidence of conflict with neighboring Web Technologies and APIs projects?

691. What is the risk appetite?

692. What are the uncertainties associated with the technology selected for the Web Technologies and APIs project?

693. What is the impact if the risk does occur?

694. What is the likely future demand of the customer?

695. Are enough people available?

696. Are tool mentors available?

697. Is the technology to be built new to your organization?

698. What is the culture of the market and the company?

699. What is Web Technologies and APIs project Risk Management?

700. Is Web Technologies and APIs project scope stable?

701. Are formal technical reviews part of this process?

702. What can Possibly Go Wrong?

703. How carefully have the potential competitors been identified?

704. Are people attending meetings and doing work?

2.35 Risk Data Sheet: Web Technologies and APIs

705. What is the duration of infection (the length of time the host is infected with the organizm) in a normal healthy human host?

706. How can hazards be reduced?

707. If it happens, what are the consequences?

708. Potential for Recurrence?

709. What are you trying to achieve (Objectives)?

710. What can YOU do?

711. Are new hazards created?

712. How reliable is the data source?

713. What were the Causes that contributed?

714. Has the most cost-effective solution been chosen?

715. What are the main opportunities available to us that you should grab while you can?

716. During work activities could hazards exist?

717. Do effective diagnostic tests exist?

718. What is the likelihood of it happening?

719. Risk of What?

720. How do you handle product safely?

721. What is the environment within which you operate (social trends, economic, community values, broad based participation, national directions etc.)?

722. Is the data sufficiently specified in terms of the type of failure being analysed, and its frequency or probability?

723. Type of Risk Identified?

724. Whom do you serve (customers)?

2.36 Procurement Management Plan: Web Technologies and APIs

725. Are all resource assumptions documented?

726. Are all payments made according to the contract(s)?

727. Are all key components of a Quality Assurance Plan present?

728. Are meeting minutes captured and sent out after meetings?

729. Are schedule deliverables actually delivered?

730. Has a Quality Assurance Plan been developed for the Web Technologies and APIs project?

731. Have activity relationships and interdependencies within tasks been adequately identified?

732. Do Web Technologies and APIs project teams & team members report on status / activities / progress?

733. Is there a Quality Management Plan?

734. Does a documented Web Technologies and APIs project organizational policy & plan (i.e. governance model) exist?

735. Is there a procurement management plan in

place?

736. Public engagement – Did you get it right?

737. Is the schedule updated on a periodic basis?

738. Are governance roles and responsibilities documented?

739. Are non-critical path items updated and agreed upon with the teams?

740. Are Web Technologies and APIs project leaders committed to this Web Technologies and APIs project full time?

741. What areas are overlooked on this Web Technologies and APIs project?

2.37 Source Selection Criteria: Web Technologies and APIs

742. What are the guidelines regarding award without discussions?

743. What is the role of counsel in the procurement process?

744. Does the evaluation of any change include an impact analysis; how will the change affect the scope, time, cost, and quality of the goods or services being provided?

745. What is the basis of an estimate and what assumptions were made?

746. What documentation should be used to support the selection decision?

747. Is the offeror pricing what is technically proposed?

748. Is This a Cost Contract?

749. What management structure does the organization consider as optimal for performing the contract?

750. When is it appropriate to conduct a preproposal conference?

751. How important is cost in the source selection

decision relative to past performance and technical considerations?

752. How should oral presentations be evaluated?

753. Will the technical evaluation factor unnecessarily force the acquisition into a higher-priced market segment?

754. Who is on the Source Selection Advisory Committee?

755. What aspects should the contracting officer brief the Web Technologies and APIs project on prior to evaluation of proposals?

756. What should clarifications include?

757. Does an evaluation need to include the identification of strengths and weaknesses?

758. How do you encourage efficiency and consistency?

759. Are types/quantities of material, facilities appropriate?

760. What benefits are accrued from issuing a DRFP in advance of issuing a final RFP?

761. Do you have designated specific forms or worksheets?

2.38 Stakeholder Management Plan: Web Technologies and APIs

762. Are software metrics formally captured, analyzed and used as a basis for other Web Technologies and APIs project estimates?

763. Who would sign off on the charter?

764. Are cause and effect determined for risks when they occur?

765. Are changes in deliverable commitments agreed to by all affected groups & individuals?

766. Are Web Technologies and APIs project team members involved in detailed estimating and scheduling?

767. Are stakeholders aware and supportive of the principles and practices of modern software estimation?

768. Have you eliminated all duplicative tasks or manual efforts, where appropriate?

769. Are changes in scope (deliverable commitments) agreed to by all affected groups & individuals?

770. Who is responsible for arranging and managing the review(s)?

771. Where does the information come from?

772. What is to be the method of release?

773. Are the appropriate IT resources adequate to meet planned commitments?

774. What is the primary function of the Activity Decomposition Decision Tree?

775. Has a provision been made to reassess Web Technologies and APIs project risks at various Web Technologies and APIs project stages?

776. Is there an issues management plan in place?

777. Have all necessary approvals been obtained?

778. Were Web Technologies and APIs project team members involved in the development of activity & task decomposition?

779. Where are the verification requirements to be documented (eg purchase order, agreement etc)?

2.39 Change Management Plan: Web Technologies and APIs

780. What will be the preferred method of delivery?

781. What are the specific target groups/audiences that will be impacted by this change?

782. Where will the funds come from?

783. How badly can information be misinterpreted?

784. How prevalent is Resistance to Change?

785. When to start change management?

786. Will the readiness criteria be met prior to the training roll out?

787. How can you best frame the message so that it addresses the audiences interests?

788. What processes are in place to manage knowledge about the Web Technologies and APIs project?

789. What do you expect the target audience to do, say, think or feel as a result of this communication?

790. Have the business unit contacts been briefed by the Web Technologies and APIs project team?

791. Who will be the change levers?

792. What are you trying to achieve as a result of communication?

793. Who is the audience for change management activities?

794. Has a training need analysis been carried out?

795. Who might be able to help us the most?

796. Who might be able to help you the most?

797. Is a training information sheet available?

798. What risks may occur upfront?

3.0 Executing Process Group: Web Technologies and APIs

799. Do Web Technologies and APIs project managers understand the organizational context for their Web Technologies and APIs projects?

800. Do the products created live up to the necessary quality?

801. How well did the chosen processes fit the needs of the Web Technologies and APIs project?

802. What is the difference between using brainstorming and the Delphi technique for risk identification?

803. Just how important is your work to the overall success of the Web Technologies and APIs project?

804. How many different communication channels does the Web Technologies and APIs project team have?

805. Is the Web Technologies and APIs project making progress in helping to achieve the set results?

806. What areas does the group agree are the biggest success on the Web Technologies and APIs project?

807. Will new hardware or software be required for servers or client machines?

808. What factors are contributing to progress or delay in the achievement of products and results?

809. What does it mean to take a systems view of a Web Technologies and APIs project?

810. What will you do to minimize the impact should a risk event occur?

811. When do you share the scorecard with managers?

812. How does Web Technologies and APIs project management relate to other disciplines?

813. How do you prevent staff are just doing busywork to pass the time?

814. Are escalated issues resolved promptly?

815. How well did the team follow the chosen processes?

816. When is the appropriate time to bring the scorecard to Board meetings?

817. What type of people would you want on your team?

3.1 Team Member Status Report: Web Technologies and APIs

818. Are the products of the organization's Web Technologies and APIs projects meeting their customer's objectives?

819. How it is to be done?

820. How does this product, good, or service meet the needs of the Web Technologies and APIs project and the organization as a whole?

821. How will Resource Planning be done?

822. Are the attitudes of staff regarding Web Technologies and APIs project work improving?

823. Does the organization have the means (staff, money, contract, etc.) to produce or to acquire the product, good, or service?

824. What specific interest groups do you have in place?

825. When a teams productivity and success depend on collaboration and the efficient flow of information, what generally fails them?

826. Is there evidence that staff is taking a more professional approach toward management of the organizations Web Technologies and APIs projects?

827. How can you make it practical?

828. The problem with Reward & Recognition Programs is that the truly deserving people all too often get left out. How can you make it practical?

829. Does every department have to have a Web Technologies and APIs project Manager on staff?

830. Are the organization's Web Technologies and APIs projects more successful over time?

831. Do you have an Enterprise Web Technologies and APIs project Management Office (EPMO)?

832. Does the product, good, or service already exist within the organization?

833. Will the staff do training or is that done by a third party?

834. Why is it to be done?

835. What is to be done?

836. How much risk is involved?

3.2 Change Request: Web Technologies and APIs

837. For which areas does this operating procedure apply?

838. Are there requirements attributes that are strongly related to the complexity and size?

839. How are the measures for carrying out the change established?

840. How can you ensure that changes have been made properly?

841. What is a Change Request Form?

842. Can you answer what happened, who did it, when did it happen, and what else will be affected?

843. How well do experienced software developers predict software change?

844. How does an organization control changes before and after software is released to a customer?

845. Describe how modifications, enhancements, defects and/or deficiencies shall be notified (e.g. Problem Reports, Change Requests etc) and managed. Detail warranty and/or maintenance periods?

846. How do team members communicate with each

other?

847. What must be taken into consideration when introducing change control programs?

848. Which requirements attributes affect the risk to reliability the most?

849. How is the change documented (format, content, storage)?

850. What needs to be communicated?

851. Why control change across the life cycle?

852. Have all related configuration items been properly updated?

853. How does a team identify the discrete elements of a configuration?

854. Who Will Perform the Change?

855. Are change requests logged and managed?

856. What has an inspector to inspect and to check?

3.3 Change Log: Web Technologies and APIs

857. Who initiated the change request?

858. Do the described changes impact on the integrity or security of the system?

859. Does the suggested change request seem to represent a necessary enhancement to the product?

860. When was the request submitted?

861. Is the submitted change a new change or a modification of a previously approved change?

862. Is the change request open, closed or pending?

863. Is the requested change request a result of changes in other Web Technologies and APIs project(s)?

864. Is this a mandatory replacement?

865. Where Do Changes Come From?

866. When was the request approved?

867. Is the change request within Web Technologies and APIs project scope?

868. How does this change affect the timeline of the schedule?

869. Will the Web Technologies and APIs project fail if the change request is not executed?

870. How does this relate to the standards developed for specific business processes?

871. How does this change affect scope?

872. Is the change backward compatible without limitations?

3.4 Decision Log: Web Technologies and APIs

873. How effective is maintaining the log at facilitating organizational learning?

874. Who will be given a copy of this document and where will it be kept?

875. What are the cost implications?

876. Which variables make a critical difference?

877. What makes you different or better than others companies selling the same thing?

878. What was the rationale for the decision?

879. What alternatives/risks were considered?

880. Meeting purpose; why does this team meet?

881. Decision-making process; how will the team make decisions?

882. How does the use a Decision Support System influence the strategies/tactics or costs?

883. What is the average size of your matters in an applicable measurement?

884. Does anything need to be adjusted?

885. How do you know when you are achieving it?

886. Is everything working as expected?

887. At what point in time does loss become unacceptable?

888. What eDiscovery problem or issue did your company set out to fix or make better?

889. How do you define success?

890. Adversarial Environment. Is your opponent open to a non-traditional workflow, or will it likely challenge anything you do?

891. It becomes critical to track and periodically revisit both operational effectiveness; Are you noticing all that you need to, and are you interpreting what you see effectively?

892. Who is the decisionmaker?

3.5 Quality Audit: Web Technologies and APIs

893. What is the collective experience of the team to be assigned to an audit?

894. How do staff know if they are doing a good job?

895. How does the organization know that its range of activities are being reviewed as rigorously and constructively as they could be?

896. Are the intentions consistent with external obligations (such as applicable laws)?

897. Can the organization demonstrate exactly how and why results were achieved?

898. How does the organization know that its risk management system is appropriately effective and constructive?

899. How is the Strategic Plan (and other plans) reviewed and revised?

900. Is the organizational structure established and each positions responsibility defined?

901. What does an analysis of the organizations staff profile suggest in terms of its planning, and how is this being addressed?

902. Is there any content that may be legally

actionable?

903. How does the organization know that its system for staff performance planning and review is appropriately effective and constructive?

904. A judgment has to be made as to whether a particular practice is good or poor or otherwise. How does one decide on a practice?

905. How are you auditing the organizations compliance with regulations?

906. How does the organization know that its security arrangements are appropriately effective and constructive?

907. What are the main things that hinder your ability to do a good job?

908. How does the organization know that the support for its staff is appropriately effective and constructive?

909. What are you trying to accomplish with this audit?

910. Are all employees including salespersons made aware that they must report all complaints received from any source for inclusion in the complaint handling system?

911. How does the organization know that the range and quality of its accommodation, catering and transportation services are appropriately effective and constructive?

912. What does an analysis of an organizations staff profile suggest in terms of its planning, and how is this being addressed?

3.6 Team Directory: Web Technologies and APIs

913. Who are your stakeholders (customers, sponsors, end users, team members)?

914. Process Decisions: Do job conditions warrant additional actions to collect job information and document on-site activity?

915. Who should receive information (all stakeholders)?

916. Contract requirements complied with?

917. Does a Web Technologies and APIs project team directory list all resources assigned to the Web Technologies and APIs project?

918. How does the team resolve conflicts and ensure tasks are completed?

919. Process Decisions: Which organizational elements and which individuals will be assigned management functions?

920. Who will write the meeting minutes and distribute?

921. Process Decisions: Are there any statutory or regulatory issues relevant to the timely execution of work?

922. When will you produce deliverables?

923. Decisions: What could be done better to improve the quality of the constructed product?

924. What are you going to deliver or accomplish?

925. Do purchase specifications and configurations match requirements?

926. How will you accomplish and manage the objectives?

927. Who will report Web Technologies and APIs project status to all stakeholders?

928. Who will be the stakeholders on your next Web Technologies and APIs project?

929. Where should the information be distributed?

930. Process Decisions: Do invoice amounts match accepted work in place?

931. Who is the Sponsor?

3.7 Team Operating Agreement: Web Technologies and APIs

932. What is your unique contribution to the organization?

933. Have you set the goals and objectives of the team?

934. Are there more than two national cultures represented by your team?

935. The method to be used in the decision making process; Will it be consensus, majority rule, or the supervisor having the final say?

936. Do you upload presentation materials in advance and test the technology?

937. How does teaming fit in with overall organizational goals and meet organizational needs?

938. Do you ask participants to close their laptops and place their mobile devices on silent on the table while the meeting is in progress?

939. Did you recap the meeting purpose, time, and expectations?

940. To whom do you deliver our services?

941. Do you vary your voice pace, tone and pitch to engage participants and gain involvement?

942. How will your group handle planned absences?

943. Are there more than two native languages represented by your team?

944. What is the number of cases currently teamed?

945. Must your members collaborate successfully to complete Web Technologies and APIs projects?

946. Resource Allocation: How will individual team members account for their time and expenses, and how will this be allocated in the team budget?

947. Do you leverage technology engagement tools group chat, polls, screen sharing, etc.?

948. Do you use a parking lot for any items that are important but outside of the agenda?

949. Do you brief absent members after they view meeting notes or listen to a recording?

950. Methodologies: How will key team processes be implemented, such as training, research, work deliverable production, review and approval processes, knowledge management, and meeting procedures?

951. What are the boundaries (organizational or geographic) within which you operate?

3.8 Team Performance Assessment: Web Technologies and APIs

952. To what degree does the teams work approach provide opportunity for members to engage in open interaction?

953. To what degree can team members meet frequently enough to accomplish the teams ends?

954. To what degree do team members agree with the goals, their relative importance, and the ways in which their achievement will be measured?

955. To what degree are the members clear on what they are individually responsible for and what they are jointly responsible for?

956. Which situations call for a more extreme type of adaptiveness in which team members actually re-define their roles?

957. To what degree are staff involved as partners in the improvement process?

958. When does the medium matter?

959. Social categorization and intergroup behaviour: Does minimal intergroup discrimination make social identity more positive?

960. If you are worried about method variance before you collect data, what sort of design elements might

you include to reduce or eliminate the threat of method variance?

961. To what degree are fresh input and perspectives systematically caught and added (for example, through information and analysis, new members, and senior sponsors)?

962. To what degree are the teams goals and objectives clear, simple, and measurable?

963. To what degree are the skill areas critical to team performance present?

964. Where to from here?

965. To what degree will team members, individually and collectively, commit time to help themselves and others learn and develop skills?

966. To what degree do members understand and articulate the same purpose without relying on ambiguous abstractions?

967. How do you encourage members to learn from each other?

968. To what degree are these categories of skills either actually or potentially represented across the membership?

969. What structural changes have you made or are you preparing to make?

970. If you have criticized someones work for method variance in your role as reviewer, what was the

circumstance?

971. Individual task proficiency and team process behavior: Whats important for team functioning?

3.9 Team Member Performance Assessment: Web Technologies and APIs

972. To what degree is the team cognizant of small wins to be celebrated along the way?

973. What variables that affect team members achievement are within your control?

974. How is assessment information achieved, stored?

975. What are the basic principles and objectives of performance measurement and assessment?

976. Where can team members go for more detailed information on performance measurement and assessment?

977. To what degree are the relative importance and priority of the goals clear to all team members?

978. What instructional strategies were developed/ incorporated (e.g., direct instruction, indirect instruction, experiential learning, independent study, interactive instruction)?

979. What types of learning are targeted (e.g., cognitive, affective, psychomotor, procedural)?

980. To what degree are the goals ambitious?

981. What are the standards or expectations for

success?

982. How effective is training that is delivered through technology-based platforms?

983. What innovations (if any) are developed to realize goals?

984. How is performance assessment used in making future award decisions including options and extend/ compete decisions?

985. How do you currently explain your results in the teams achievement?

986. How do you start collaborating?

987. How does your team work together?

988. What happens if a team member disagrees with the Job Expectations?

3.10 Issue Log: Web Technologies and APIs

989. Are there too many who have an interest in some aspect of your work?

990. Who have you worked with in past, similar initiatives?

991. Do you have members of your team responsible for certain stakeholders?

992. Why Multiple Evaluators?

993. What is a change?

994. What is a Stakeholder?

995. Is there an important stakeholder who is actively opposed and will not receive messages?

996. What is the impact on the risks?

997. What is the stakeholders level of authority?

998. Why not more evaluators?

999. What is the status of the issue?

1000. Is the Issue Log kept in a safe place?

1001. Why Do you Manage Human Resources?

1002. What does the stakeholder need from the team?

1003. Are they needed?

1004. What steps can you take for positive relationships?

1005. Who do you turn to if you have questions?

1006. What is the impact on the Business Case?

1007. Who is involved as you identify stakeholders?

4.0 Monitoring and Controlling Process Group: Web Technologies and APIs

1008. Where is the Risk in the Web Technologies and APIs project?

1009. Did the Web Technologies and APIs project team have enough people to execute the Web Technologies and APIs project plan?

1010. What departments are involved in its daily operation?

1011. Who needs to be engaged upfront to ensure use of results?

1012. What kinds of things in particular are you looking for data on?

1013. Is the schedule for the set products being met?

1014. Just how important is your work to the overall success of the Web Technologies and APIs project?

1015. How will staff learn how to use the deliverables?

1016. How Can You Monitor Progress?

1017. What are the goals of the program?

1018. Are the necessary foundations in place to ensure the sustainability of the results of the programme?

1019. Do the partners have sufficient financial capacity to keep up the benefits produced by the programme?

1020. How were collaborations developed, and how are they sustained?

1021. Did you implement the program as designed?

1022. Is the verbiage used appropriate and understandable?

4.1 Project Performance Report: Web Technologies and APIs

1023. To what degree are sub-teams possible or necessary?

1024. To what degree does the team possess adequate membership to achieve its ends?

1025. To what degree is there a sense that only the team can succeed?

1026. To what degree does the team's purpose contain themes that are particularly meaningful and memorable?

1027. To what degree do team members feel that the purpose of the team is important, if not exciting?

1028.　　To what degree can the cognitive capacity of individuals accommodate the flow of information?

1029. To what degree will the approach capitalize on and enhance the skills of all team members in a manner that takes into consideration other demands on members of the team?

1030. To what degree can the team measure progress against specific goals?

1031. To what degree do team members understand one another's roles and skills?

1032. What is in it for you?

1033. To what degree will new and supplemental skills be introduced as the need is recognized?

1034. To what degree does the team's work approach provide opportunity for members to engage in fact-based problem solving?

1035. To what degree does the information network provide individuals with the information they require?

1036. To what degree do the structures of the formal organization motivate task- relevant behavior and facilitate task completion?

1037. Next Steps?

1038. To what degree do individual skills and abilities match task demands?

1039. How is the data used?

1040. To what degree does the informal organization make use of individual resources and meet individual needs?

4.2 Variance Analysis: Web Technologies and APIs

1041. When, during the last four quarters, did a primary business event occur causing a fluctuation?

1042. What is the incurrence of actual indirect costs in excess of budgets, by element of expense?

1043. How do you verify authorization to proceed with all authorized work?

1044. Historical experience?

1045. Why are standard cost systems used?

1046. What is the actual cost of work performed?

1047. What does a favorable labor efficiency variance mean?

1048. Wbs elements contractually specified for reporting of status to the organization (lowest level only)?

1049. Who are responsible for the establishment of budgets and assignment of resources for overhead performance?

1050. How does the use of a single conversion element (rather than the traditional labor and overhead elements) affect standard costing?

1051. Contemplated overhead expenditure for each period based on the best information currently is available?

1052. What are the actual costs to date?

1053. Favorable or Unfavorable Variance?

1054. Are there changes in the direct base to which overhead costs are allocated?

1055. What types of services and expense are shared between business segments?

1056. Are the actual costs used for variance analysis reconcilable with data from the accounting system?

4.3 Earned Value Status: Web Technologies and APIs

1057. How much is it going to cost by the finish?

1058. If earned value management (EVM) is so good in determining the true status of a Web Technologies and APIs project and Web Technologies and APIs project its completion, why is it that hardly any one uses it in information systems related Web Technologies and APIs projects?

1059. Validation is a process of ensuring that the developed system will actually achieve the stakeholders desired outcomes; Are you building the right product? What do you validate?

1060. Where is Evidence-based Earned Value in your organization reported?

1061. When is it going to finish?

1062. Where are your problem areas?

1063. Are you hitting your Web Technologies and APIs projects targets?

1064. How does this compare with other Web Technologies and APIs projects?

1065. Verification is a process of ensuring that the developed system satisfies the stakeholders agreements and specifications; Are you building the product right? What do you verify?

1066. What is the unit of forecast value?

1067. Earned Value can be used in almost any Web Technologies and APIs project situation and in almost any Web Technologies and APIs project environment. It may be used on large Web Technologies and APIs projects, medium sized Web Technologies and APIs projects, tiny Web Technologies and APIs projects (in cut-down form), complex and simple Web Technologies and APIs projects and in any market sector. Some people, of course, know all about earned value, they have used it for years - but perhaps not as effectively as they could have?

4.4 Risk Audit: Web Technologies and APIs

1068. Does the adoption of a business risk audit approach change internal control documentation and testing practices?

1069. Are Audit Program Plans Risk-Adjusted?

1070. What are the differences and similarities between strategic and operational risks in your organization?

1071. What are Risks and How do you Manage Them?

1072. Have you considered the health and safety of everyone in the organization and do you meet work health and safety regulations?

1073. Are risk management strategies documented?

1074. Is there a clear procedure for reporting accidents/injuries?

1075. Does Willful Intent Modify Risk-Based Auditing?

1076. What are the risks that could stop us from achieving our objectives?

1077. Is a software Web Technologies and APIs project management tool available?

1078. How do you compare to other jurisdictions

when managing the risk of ....?

1079. Who is responsible for what?

1080. Extending the discussion on the halo effect, to what extent are auditors able to build skepticism in evidence review?

1081. Do you have a consistent repeatable process that is actually used?

1082. Do you record and file all audits?

1083. From an empirical perspective, does the business risk approach lead to a more effective audit, or simply to increased consulting revenue detrimental to audit rigor?

1084. Is your organization able to present documentary evidence in support of compliance?

1085. Do you have an understanding of insurance claims processes?

1086. Mitigation -how can you avoid the risk?

1087. Are some people working on multiple Web Technologies and APIs projects?

4.5 Contractor Status Report: Web Technologies and APIs

1088. Describe how often regular updates are made to the proposed solution. Are these regular updates included in the standard maintenance plan?

1089. Who can list a Web Technologies and APIs project as company experience, the company or a previous employee of the company?

1090. What process manages the contracts?

1091. What was the final actual cost?

1092. What was the actual budget or estimated cost for your companys services?

1093. Are there contractual transfer concerns?

1094. What is the average response time for answering a support call?

1095. How long have you been using the services?

1096. What was the budget or estimated cost for your companys services?

1097. What are the minimum and optimal bandwidth requirements for the proposed soluiton?

1098. If applicable; describe your standard schedule for new software version releases. Are new software version releases included in the standard maintenance plan?

1099. What was the overall budget or estimated cost?

1100. How is Risk Transferred?

1101. How does the proposed individual meet each requirement?

4.6 Formal Acceptance: Web Technologies and APIs

1102. Is formal acceptance of the Web Technologies and APIs project product documented and distributed?

1103. Have all comments been addressed?

1104. What function(s) does it fill or meet?

1105. Does it do what client said it would?

1106. Who would use it?

1107. Who supplies data?

1108. How does your team plan to obtain formal acceptance on your Web Technologies and APIs project?

1109. Was the client satisfied with the Web Technologies and APIs project results?

1110. What lessons were learned about your Web Technologies and APIs project management methodology?

1111. What can you do better next time?

1112. What features, practices, and processes proved to be strengths or weaknesses?

1113. Was the sponsor/customer satisfied?

1114. Was the Web Technologies and APIs project goal achieved?

1115. Was business value realized?

1116. What is the Acceptance Management Process?

1117. Was the Web Technologies and APIs project work done on time, within budget, and according to specification?

1118. What was done right?

1119. General estimate of the costs and times to complete the Web Technologies and APIs project?

1120. How well did the team follow the methodology?

1121. Do you buy pre-configured systems or build your own configuration?

5.0 Closing Process Group: Web Technologies and APIs

1122. Were the outcomes different from those planned?

1123. Are there funding or time constraints?

1124. Is the Web Technologies and APIs project Funded?

1125. Were decisions made in a timely manner?

1126. What is the overall risk of the Web Technologies and APIs project to the organization?

1127. How Will You Know You Did It?

1128. What is the amount of funding and what Web Technologies and APIs project phases are funded?

1129. What were the actual outcomes?

1130. Based on your Web Technologies and APIs project communication management plan, what worked well?

1131. Did you do what you said you were going to do?

1132. Was the schedule met?

1133. Were risks identified and mitigated?

1134. Were escalated issues resolved promptly?

1135. What could be done to improve the process?

1136. What could have been improved?

1137. How critical is the Web Technologies and APIs project success to the success of the organization?

1138. What areas does the group agree are the biggest success on the Web Technologies and APIs project?

1139. What was learned?

5.1 Procurement Audit: Web Technologies and APIs

1140. Are prices always included on the purchase order?

1141. Are cases of double payment duly prevented and corrected?

1142. Are approvals needed if changes are made in the quantity or specification of the original purchase requisition?

1143. Do you learn from benchmarking your own practices with international standards?

1144. Were the tender documents comprehensive, transparent and free from restrictions or conditions which would discriminate against certain suppliers?

1145. Was a formal review of tenders received undertaken?

1146. Is the departments procurement function/unit well organized?

1147. Are proper financing arrangements taken?

1148. Is there a form specified for bids?

1149. Does the procurement process compile basic procurement information such as how much is bought and spend with individual suppliers?

1150. Does the procurement unit have sound commercial awareness and knowledge of suppliers and the market?

1151. Is there time waste during tendering?

1152. Are all purchase orders accounted for?

1153. Has guidelines been set up for how the procurement function/unit should carry out its procurements?

1154. Is the procurement process fully digitalized?

1155. Was the formal review of requests to participate or evaluation of bids correctly undertaken?

1156. When you set social or environmental conditions for the performance of the contract, were these compatible with the law and was adequate information given to the candidates?

1157. Has the organization fulfilled its obligations related to the payment of social security contributions and taxes?

1158. Were no tenders presented after the time limit accepted?

1159. Does the strategy ensure that appropriate controls are in place to ensure propriety and regularity in delivery?

5.2 Contract Close-Out: Web Technologies and APIs

1160. How is the contracting office notified of the automatic contract close-out?

1161. Have all acceptance criteria been met prior to final payment to contractors?

1162. Have all contracts been completed?

1163. What is Capture Management?

1164. Have all contract records been included in the Web Technologies and APIs project archives?

1165. Parties: Who is Involved?

1166. A change in knowledge?

1167. Have all contracts been closed?

1168. Are the signers the authorized officials?

1169. How/When Used ?

1170. Parties: Authorized?

1171. A change in circumstances?

1172. Was the contract sufficiently clear so as not to result in numerous disputes and misunderstandings?

1173. Has each contract been audited to verify acceptance and delivery?

1174. A change in attitude or behavior?

1175. What happens to the recipient of services?

1176. Was the contract complete without requiring numerous changes and revisions?

1177. How does it work?

1178. Was the contract type appropriate?

1179. Why Outsource?

5.3 Project or Phase Close-Out: Web Technologies and APIs

1180. Were messages directly related to the release strategy or phases of the Web Technologies and APIs project?

1181. Was the user/client satisfied with the end product?

1182. What Security Considerations needed to be addressed during the Procurement Life Cycle?

1183. Is the lesson significant, valid, and applicable?

1184. Which changes might a stakeholder be required to make as a result of the Web Technologies and APIs project?

1185. What are the informational communication needs for each stakeholder?

1186. If you were the Web Technologies and APIs project sponsor, how would you determine which Web Technologies and APIs project team(s) and/or individuals deserve recognition?

1187. In addition to assessing whether the Web Technologies and APIs project was successful, it is equally critical to analyze why it was or was not fully successful. Are you including this?

1188. Did the delivered product meet the specified

requirements and goals of the Web Technologies and APIs project?

1189. What process was planned for managing issues/ risks?

1190. Can the lesson learned be replicated?

1191. What were the desired outcomes?

1192. Does the lesson describe a function that would be done differently the next time?

1193. Who is Responsible for Award Close-out?

1194. Who exerted influence that has positively affected or negatively impacted the Web Technologies and APIs project?

1195. What can you do better next time, and what specific actions can you take to improve?

1196. What was the preferred delivery mechanism?

1197. Have business partners been involved extensively, and what data was required for them?

5.4 Lessons Learned: Web Technologies and APIs

1198. Is the lesson based on actual Web Technologies and APIs project experience rather than on independent research?

1199. What was the geopolitical history during the origin of the organization and at the time of task input?

1200. How objective was the collection of data?

1201. How useful was the format and content of the Web Technologies and APIs project Status Report to you?

1202. How well was Web Technologies and APIs project status communicated throughout your involvement in the Web Technologies and APIs project?

1203. Are there any data that you have overlooked in identifying lessons?

1204. How satisfied are you with your involvement in the development and/or review of the Web Technologies and APIs project Scope during Web Technologies and APIs project Initiation and Planning?

1205. Who Needs to Learn Lessons?

1206. Was the Change Control process properly implemented to manage changes to Cost, Scope, Schedule, or Quality?

1207. What worked well or did not work well, either for this Web Technologies and APIs project or for the Web Technologies and APIs project team?

1208. How complete and timely were the materials you were provided to decide whether to proceed from one Web Technologies and APIs project lifecycle phase to the next?

1209. How well did the Web Technologies and APIs project Manager respond to questions or comments related to the Web Technologies and APIs project?

1210. How timely were Progress Reports provided to the Web Technologies and APIs project Manager by Team Members?

1211. How was the quality of products/processes assured?

1212. How closely did deliverables match what was defined within the Web Technologies and APIs project Scope?

1213. What was the methodology behind successful learning experiences, and how might they be applied to the broader challenge of the organizations knowledge management?

1214. Did the Web Technologies and APIs project improve the team members reputations, skills, personal development?

1215. Were the Web Technologies and APIs project Objectives met (If not, briefly explain what wasnt met)?

Index

necessary   38, 50, 53, 61, 81, 94, 97, 118, 157, 172, 175, 190, 193, 199, 217, 219

needed   17, 20, 34, 51, 71, 73, 75, 106-107, 155, 157, 166, 216, 233, 237

negatively   238

negotiate   94

negotiated   102

neither 1

Network   4, 141-142, 220

Neutral 12, 17, 24, 35, 47, 56, 68, 79

nonlinear   163

normal 72, 183

notice 1, 113

noticing   202

notified   173, 197, 235

number   23, 34, 39, 46, 55, 67, 77, 102, 138, 161, 180, 209, 242

numerous   235-236

objective   8, 36, 107, 112, 180, 239

objectives   19, 21, 24, 28, 52, 54, 70, 75, 80, 94, 97, 115, 147, 162, 172, 178, 183, 195, 207-208, 211, 213, 225, 241

observe   169

observed   63

obsolete   86

obstacles   22, 139, 149, 158

obstruct   110

obtain 95, 229

obtained   27, 42, 106, 190

obvious   97

obviously   13

occurring   62, 106, 178

occurs 21, 71, 113, 179

offerings   48, 62

offeror 187

office   196, 235

officer 188

officials 235

offshore   122

onboarding   154

one-time   8

ongoing   42, 60, 77, 149

online 11

on-site 206

271

Lightning Source UK Ltd.
Milton Keynes UK
UKHW040702191118
332582UK00011B/362/P

BIN TRAVELER FORM

Cut By: _ashly_   _27_   Qty _29_   Date _06-16-26_

Scanned By: _____ Qty _____ Date _____

Scanned Batch ID's

_____

Notes / Exceptions